TABL

CHAPTER ONE: GOD'S CHILD OR SATAN'S ANGEL

The problem with being smart is that you remember what has happened in your life, no matter how good, or bad. Sure, you do well in school and impress a few friends watching jeopardy, but what happens when your memories are nightmares that you want to forget but you can't? What happens then?

The answer is you make yourself forget. No matter what the cost, you make yourself forget. The catch with doing this is when you forget the past you also forget the good things that have taken place. More importantly, you forget how to be good. This is what I did... this is how I became a monster.

Ironically, my first memory is one of my happiest. It was before I could even talk, but the memory is vivid as yesterday. My mother and I are walking on a path in a park together. Well, my mother is walking while I enjoy the ride from my baby harness on her back. It is right before sundown on a perfect day. Suddenly, the most dreadfully impossible thing happened to me. I can no longer see my mother's angelic face. I never felt safe unless I was in the presence of her eternal smile. I cry out in the best way I know to be delivered from this divine separation. Then, like my guardian angel, she brings me back to her loving embrace. Everything is okay once again. Everything will always be okay as long as I just stay here.

I didn't stay there, however. In fact, I soon went to the farthest place from there I could possibly go. As if this were a reverse foreshadowing, I was ripped instantly from the loving arms of an angel into the darkest abyss of hell. Although it started as a fairytale, my dream ended in a nightmare. I have met many evil people in my life who were empty and dark on the inside.

In prison I've come across thieves, liars, cheats, murderers, rapists, serial killers, and even child molesters, but the first face of evil I ever encountered in this life was my father. The sad thing is that I look just like him. Sometimes this is something I still regret, even to this day. How can you try and forget the face of a demon when every time you look into a mirror you see him staring back at you? Never saying a word, he looks at you with a smirk on his face. I hated him. I hated him because he took the most precious thing on this earth from me. This was the only thing that ever made me feel safe. He took my mother from me.

He didn't take her life, because my mother is still fine and healthy to this day. She was as good as dead for the longest time, because he took her soul. Without it, she would never be the same. It is weird how as a male human being you bestow responsibilities upon yourself. Even as a small child I would do this very thing. Not even old enough to understand the concept of what I was partaking in, I still had my special duties as man of the house. In retrospect, it is completely absurd for a 2 or 3 year old child to be a protector for his full grown mother. At the time, however, I didn't realize this, and brought the responsibility upon myself to keep my family from danger. I state this so that you can get an idea of how much I blamed myself for failing in the unobtainable task of protecting my mother from the abuse afflicted on her by my father. Later on in my life this sense of responsibility will again be assigned to me. Just as before, I will fail to reach this unreasonable goal yet again.

I was born and raised for the first three years of my life in Ojai, California, which is in Ventura County. When I think back, I still remember the layout of the house, and even where every piece of furniture was placed in my childhood home. The house reminds me of the cottage from "Hansel & Gretel". On the outside, our home seemed like it was all sugar plums and candy canes with a perfect family to boot. On the inside of the cottage, there was anything but sugar & spice. It was a dungeon where damned souls went to perish at the hands of a monster. My mother has had many titles in her life. This great country of ours would call her a citizen. To me, she is a mother. At her current job, she is known as a boss. My father, on the other hand, thought of her in only one aspect… "Property". In a way the word slave could also be used. She was his property, and he had no qualms about letting her know that fact at anytime. Of course, it takes a big man to beat up on a woman who is physically weaker and can't defend herself. I think Webster actually uses this quality in his great dictionary to define the word "Man". I don't know if my mother did this to protect me, or if my father did it to hide from me how much of a coward he really was, but for whatever the reason, they would always do their fighting behind closed doors in their bedroom. That is the location where my father would show his property that she was just that. They took no precautions to ensure that I couldn't hear the constant yelling. I guess this was okay, as long as I didn't witness the abominable acts that took place with my eyes. What they didn't know was that I did see what went on in that room. I witnessed every single act of violence perpetrated on my mother, and to this day I still remember most of them. I have always remembered, even though for awhile I purposely locked away those memories in the recesses of my brain due to the emotional psychosis that it brought upon me. Now I have recently brought them back to the surface in order for those memories to no longer hold any power over me. How did I see through bedroom walls? As much as I wish I had that super power, the answer is I didn't. I was able to spy through the keyhole of the door, giving me a front row seat to the most evil and twisted circus ever to perform under any big top tent. That is how I first witnessed the perfect face of evil. That was when I first looked into the eyes of the devil and couldn't look away.

I remember every time my mother was sent to the hospital. I blamed myself. Every time she was punched in the face by a fully-grown man, I blamed myself. Every broken nose I felt like the blood was on my hands. Why? Simply, I wasn't doing my job as a protector. I wasn't stopping my mother from being abused when I should have been. I wasn't protecting the most precious thing in my life when she needed me the most. I was a failure. I was three years old and a complete failure already in life. How can I live up to any of my expectations when I failed so miserably at the simplest task of keeping my family safe? This was just the beginning of the cracks in the foundation of my life, but it definitely was a big one.

All I could think about was how weak and pathetic of a person I was. While my mother is being used in a science experiment on how to tenderize human meat, all I do is sit on the couch doing nothing to stop it. What a useless person I was. Believe it or not, I actually used to feel this way about the whole situation, and I really blamed myself for not helping my mother. The problem with that logic is this, "I was just a kid!" Yet at the time I didn't realize this and continued to blame myself, growing more and more depressed through most of my ongoing life.

This time in my life was definitely the catalyst used by the devil to jump start my ruin. The very first stones were laid in what would become my own personal Great Wall of China. Only this wall was not used to protect a kingdom. It was used to guard a scared little boy from being hurt by anyone who dared to betray his trust as everyone else had done before. This wall kept out emotions, whether they were good or bad. Why would I never mind both positive and negative emotions? The answer to this question is simple. Emotions are weaknesses. Weaknesses were exploited by people to hurt you, so I couldn't afford to have weaknesses and run the chance of somebody hurting me again.

With every punch to my mother's face, my father chipped away a part of my humanity. The chips were small to the point where they could barely be measured with a microscope. Chip by chip, and year after year, these pieces of my soul were hacked away one piece at a time. Sooner or later the mound turned into a hill, and then the hill turned into a mountain. Before I knew it, a complete psychotic breakdown had happened in my mind and I lost any sense of direction or sanity.

For years I looked back on my early childhood and despised my father for what he made me a monster who couldn't love or feel. He was the reason I became a sociopath. It was entirely his fault. He caused all the pain in my life, at this time and forever after. In fact, every person I hurt mentally or physically wasn't my fault, either. It wasn't me that ruined my life; it was that maniac that beat up my mother in front of my face. He force-fed me the evil that poisoned my soul. Well, the excuse was good while it lasted. Up until the time I had to own up to my own actions and stop blaming others, it was the perfect excuse. I found the perfect scapegoat this side of Jesus Christ and the Pharisees. Who could blame me for the way I turned out when I had a drug addicted, alcoholic, violent psycho as a father? Most people would say I never really had a chance. Heck, I said it myself for years.

CHAPTER TWO: MY BLACK SOUL'S BIRTH

The beatings by my father had become one too frequent. The hospital trips came a little too often for my mother to stand anymore. Many attempts to leave my father were made, but each try only ended in failure. How can someone leave when they have nowhere to go? How can you run away when you have nobody else to help? One of my mother's attempts to leave resulted in my father literally trying to kidnap me and my sister. You wonder, what makes a person stay through such hell? Why do people with the battered wife syndrome subject themselves to this kind of violence on a daily basis? I would watch movies about slavery and swear up and down that if I was in the same situation I would never let anyone treat me like that. Somehow you do it out of a sick and twisted sense of love. Maybe my biological father held the safety of me and my sister over my mother's head, promising if she left him we would be hurt even worse. Like most bad times in my life, I blocked it out, including being kidnapped. At least, I thought my mind would just block it out and that would be the end of it. What was really happening was the steady and rapid growth of a volcano starting to erupt. Even though it took many years to finally blow, this volcano would make Yellowstone National Park look like a bubble inside a bottle of soda.

Finally my mother was faced with only one option, she had to leave. She not only had to leave and run far away from my father, but she had to literally disappear completely from the face of the earth. My mother placed herself into a self-imposed witness protection program. You have to understand how risky it was for her to implement a plan of such magnitude. If she didn't bury herself far enough away where he couldn't find her even with his best efforts, the backlash of violence would be unprecedented. More than likely, it would have been a fatal mistake on my mom's part. We had to disappear like a C.I.A. ghost. We didn't exist anymore. She could leave no clues and absolutely no trail as to where we were headed. Thank God, my mom executed this plan flawlessly until the heat of my father's anger cooled down. Maybe my mom thanks God for executing this plan flawlessly. Soon the building blocks of my mother's new life were beginning to be put into place. It was time to let go of all that had happened in the past and focus on the promising new future that lay on our horizon. Everything seemed fine and my life was looking up for once. The bad thing is this Camelot would be cursed just as the first Camelot was. Instead of this being a new horizon for me, it was actually the calm before the storm.

When I was around five years old, my mother met my dad. Even though technically we aren't related by blood, and despite the hell-on-earth beginning of our relationship, he is the person I think of when I hear the word dad. We didn't start out that way, however. My dad's life before my family was anything but pleasant. A lifetime of mistrust and pain culminated with a debilitating addiction to heroine and all opiate derived narcotics in general. The thing about my dad is that he is a very nice man when he is on drugs. It is when he is off of them that he becomes less than cordial, you could say. A word that would describe him is "punishment", and I sure received a lot of it from him.

If you label what was going on as punishment for behaving badly as a kid, then nothing seemed to be wrong, or out of the ordinary in my life. If I would give it that label, then you can convince yourself that what is happening to you is a normal thing that all parents do to their children. The truth is it wasn't punishment, no matter how much I wanted to pull that veil over my mind's eye. The correct clinical terminology would name it "Physical and Mental Child Abuse". As much as I didn't want that to be fact, in reality that is exactly what was going on. It is weird because for many years I just blocked that time out of my thoughts completely. It wasn't until I was forced to deal with my past that I finally had a clear view of what happened in my early life. At the time, even though a part of me on the surface called what was going on punishment, deep down in the recesses of my heart I knew it was anything but punishment.

One night in the fifth grade I was listening to my radio before I went to sleep. I always listened to my radio before I fell asleep. The reason was because I was afraid of silence. There was an evil in that house, and I couldn't stand to be alone with it. One night I was told to turn off my radio. Being too scared to do so, I pleaded if I could leave it on. After a few times going back and forth, the radio ended up being smashed across the side of my head. A few days later we were all sitting around the dinner table waiting to eat when my grandmother came over to visit. When she gave my sister a hello hug, my sister immediately winced in pain. Upon further investigation, my grandmother discovered that my sister was covered in bruises on the entire back side of her body. When confronted about this, my dad simply stated, "I did a good job didn't I"? Something horrible immediately came to my realization at that moment. My sister was being beaten also. I wasn't protecting my sister just as I had failed to protect my mother. Once again, I felt like I was a complete and utter failure, and on top of that, a waste of a human being. Why was I so pathetic? I knew at the time that if I let myself be beat on a regular basis, then my father wouldn't take out his anger on the rest of my family. By doing this and allowing myself to be beaten, I was protecting them from receiving the same violent assaults. Witnessing this scene made me realize that my plan was not working at all. I blamed myself once again, only to place the whole blame as a consequence to my failed actions. It was my entire fault that this happened to my sister. As a last ditch effort the next day at school I tried to redeem myself. There was still one thing I could do to protect my sister. Before school even started I walked into the main office and asked to speak with the school counselor. I thought that when I informed him of the abuse going on at home he would surely swoop in like a knight in shining armor to finally put an end to all my nightmares. My sister and I being rescued was last thing that would happen that day. The most vivid memory in my entire life was the response I got from my school counselor after I told him of the abuse suffered by my family. These were his exact words, "There is nothing I can do about it, and the best thing for you to do is pretend it never happened". Pretend it never happened. This was the sum of my last hope being shattered right in front of my eyes forever.

I remember thinking only that I hated that man. I remember thinking I hated my step father. I hated my mom for making me take care of my sister, because it wasn't my job in the first place. What did she expect me to do other than fail miserably? I hated my sister for making me take care of her. I hated my father, and I hated the entire world. I completely and utterly hated everyone I had ever known. I hated my life to the point that it made me sick. All I felt was an overpowering hate inside me. Most of all, I hated the wretched filth that I saw in the mirror. Everything from that moment on was dead inside of me. I no longer felt real emotions. That was the day that my soul turned black.

CHAPTER THREE: CAUGHT & DEATH OF GUARDIAN

Why do people become drug addicts? What causes them to forsake all they have to use drugs? What would cause a mother to abandon her child in place of a chemical? How could a man come to the point of murdering another human being to steal the money needed to get high? The answer, being a complete paradox in itself, is actually very simple. For some reason, it always boils down to these two options: it is either how drugs make you feel, or what they make you not feel that would cause a person to forsake all that they know.

Being high for the first time was the greatest feeling in my life. I never felt so in control of my own destiny. I felt like a king who possessed absolute power over humanity. I knew nothing good or bad could happen in my life when I was on drugs because I controlled what my reality was. On drugs I felt invincible. When before all I felt was fear and pain. I was feeling true power as opposed to only knowing weakness and tears. For the first time in my life I knew what being in control over this world really felt like. When coming to this crossroads in my life, I made a vow to never feel any other way ever again.

From that point on, I was high all the time if I could help it. It was a pretty good system I had going on for awhile. All through Jr. High and into my freshman year of high school nothing really bothered me. Life was constant fun every day I was alive. The real reason nothing bothered me and I was having so much fun was that nothing could bother me, even if I wanted it too. I felt nothing and my mind was constantly numb. All the pain and suffering that I had gone through was completely gone. As far as I was concerned, those bad memories were done forever, because I would just be high forever. I thought the hurricane of my past life was over. I would no longer have to think about those nightmare times again, because I would always be high and never think about anything ever again. The truth of the matter was that I was standing smack dab in the middle of the eye of the storm. It was about to get way worse before my life got any better.

My parents started to notice something was different with me. Upon a closer look into my behavior, it was easy to tell I had become addicted to drugs. This revelation of my new life style choice was met with a blitzkrieg attack to immediately nip this problem in the bud. The problem with that strategy was that years earlier I had made up my mind to shun every authority figure throughout my remaining life. The unstoppable force had met the immovable object, and the ensuing war caused by this would leave years of destruction in its wake.

I was commanded to immediately stop doing drugs cold turkey. I was to submit to random drug testing and a flashlight check of the dilation in my pupils every time I left or returned to the house. On top of this, I was ordered to attend psychological therapy sessions on a weekly basis. I guess they were supposed to fix whatever was broken inside my mind. They didn't know there wasn't a mind to fix. My answer to this ultimatum was a verbal yes, along with nodding my head. On the inside, I had no intention whatsoever to even consider not doing drugs. Due to the fact that I had obviously thrown their ultimatum into a mud puddle and rubbed it in their faces a period of mutual hatred began between our two parties.

One night I wouldn't submit to my mother's request for an eye check. In fact, I had decided that I would never do one again. I also let my mother know that I would not be doing anything else she ever told me to do again, either. By then my anger was already borderline psychotic, so I'm not sure if what happened next was my fault or hers. Her next move was to grab a butcher knife and point it at me, to let me know she would stab me if I didn't get in line. Having absolutely no respect for her and even less fear, I didn't blink an eyelash to her bluff of a threat. That's when she did something unexpected-she tried to stab me in my body. Had I grown so out of control that my mother would stab her own son to end the torment he was bringing upon her? Who did she think I was, some punk that is going to sit back and let anyone threaten me with a knife, even if it was my own mother? Did she think this was actually supposed to scare me? Was she going to go through with stabbing her son? Then when I looked into her eyes, I could see that she was serious about ending my life. You can always look into someone's eyes and tell if they are really capable of evil. I knew my mom, at this particular moment in time, was more than capable a hundred times over. There was only one thing for me to do which was to protect myself at any cost.

As fast as I could strike I grabbed her wrist, holding the knife to keep it at a safe distance. I then grabbed her whole arm and hyper-extended her elbow and shoulder in the wrong direction. After I knew the pain had taken effect from bending her ligaments and joints in the opposite direction, I then took out her knee out from underneath her by forcing it to bend with my foot. The only thing left for me to do was slam her on the kitchen floor with swift and brutal power. Once she was pinned down and completely subdued, I continued to crank her arm in the wrong direction until I could tell that there was no more fight left in her.

Hand to hand combat has always come naturally to me, even when I use it against my own mother. I did it without even flinching or a second thought of holding myself back. I was a prodigy of violence. I loved the fact that this was true about me and savored every minute of it. Nothing made me happier than hurting people. Not even drugs could compare to the joy that it brought to my soul. A couple of minutes after this started to happen my dad came in and broke us up. It was then that I realized just how easy and fun beating up my own mother was to me. Deep down a part of me realized also that this was not normal feelings human beings should have. I knew these sick and twisted thoughts brought me pleasure. It made me realize that my limits for hurting other humans was growing smaller and smaller every passing second. I didn't see this stopping anytime soon. At that time, I felt a fear of myself that I had never felt before. I knew I couldn't stop, and I wouldn't stop myself. In this moment in my life I had not yet completely turned my mind over to the dark side. What I had just accomplished greatly disturbed me, so decided to give turning my life around one more try.

The next year many good and stable things came into my life. This helped build a shelter around my shattered past. I decided to give being a Christian an honest try. My mother had dragged me to Sunday church services in the past, so I knew if I wanted to turn my life around that was a good place to start. At that same time, the mother of one of my good friends took me under her wing. She became a mentor to me, and for the first time ever I had a mother figure to look up to. I did quit doing drugs. However, I didn't quit drinking, because even normal people still drink, right? My problems were far from solved, but at least my life seemed to be on the right track for once. This is another part of the story where gloomy, foreshadowing thunder clouds enter just above the horizon.

CHAPTER FOUR: LEAVEN OF THE PHARISEES

I was really buying into all this jargon that the church was drilling into my head. I trusted these people, mainly because they seemed to be perfect. Seemed, was the operative word in the previous sentence. On the outside of the cup, my church seemed like it was full of true holy people of God. On the inside of the cup, they were anything but holy. They should be defined as self-centered hypocrites who could care less about spreading the message of God. One by one, everyone's secrets that were hiding in the dark became visible in the light of truth. One by one, everyone's true nature was shown to anyone looking upon their character. One by one, the self-righteous dominos fell down in disgrace.

The first rumor that got out was that the pastor was having an affair with the wife of one of the head deacons. This ignited a civil war in the church between members who felt betrayed by the pastor, and those who stood loyal to their spiritual leader. The meanest and nastiest things were said to fellow church members throughout this entire ordeal. The few members who knew acting in this way was not godly behavior moved to other churches. All the while, the larger batch of bad apples stayed to rot the remaining love in the church member's hearts. I tried to not to let this whole situation bother me, but now looking back on it, I know it affected me greatly in a negative way.

I was already riding the fence as to whether I would choose allegiance to good or to complete evil as my presiding lifestyle. After I figured out what church was really all about, I knew it was full of fake and evil people. When I realized this, there was no longer a fence to ride. People were evil, whether they pretended not to be, or if they openly professed it to the world. The world was evil, and I was a perfect fit along with it.

Why go to church when the people who attend church are worse than the people who never set foot into a church sanctuary? From that point on, I completely detached myself from anything called religion. After all, I didn't need all those negative influences in my life. I knew if I wanted to be a better person I had to stay away from church. That was the place where you find the most evil people in your community. That experience definitely affected me in a negative way, because this is what my definition of church had become.

It wasn't hard withdrawing my membership from the hypocrites club. I still had a very sturdy and positive role model in my friend's mother. She showed me the first glimpse at how a selfless unconditional love manifests itself in the real world. When you posses that kind of love, it gives you a real reason to live your life to the fullest. It makes you seek out and obtain goals to make yourself a better person. One of the main reasons kids these days have no motivation to make a future for themselves is because they have no real source of unconditional parent-child love. Now I actually knew what that type of love really felt like. I finally had a reason to live… and then it was taken from me just as fast as I received it. I learned that she had a very aggressive form of cancer, and died only months after I was first told about it.

One of the most indescribably agonizing pains you will ever feel in life is the first time a loved one passes away. Up until it happens to you personally, you have no idea as to the tsunami that is about to hit. You can try and imagine the despair it will bring.

You can even try and prepare yourself for the hit so the emotions aren't as strong when the true event really happens. Even the most thorough preparation in this area is the second most futile thing a human can attempt besides working your way to heaven. When that monster of sadness is let out of its cage and unleashed on your heart, it is almost enough to kill you, too. When this hit me, I was no exception. Any small, flickering light of love that was left burning in my soul was extinguished for good by a simple cancer cell that wouldn't stop dividing.

The next year of my life was filled with drugs, parties, and more drugs with more parties. On the outside, I was having the time of my life and I never seemed happier. Inside I was just trying to move so fast and stay so numb that I didn't have to think. I could never be left alone with my thoughts from this point on. Going to that place was too dark and painful to bear even for a couple of seconds. Every once in awhile, out of some sadistic need to punish myself, I would unlock the door to my mind and peek in at the nightmare. What was the nightmare? It wasn't a horrible monster chasing me in the dark. It wasn't some bad memory haunting my every waking moment. It was a single thought that haunted me. More than a thought it was a belief... my belief of the evil reality of life.

Those beliefs were simple and yet the hardest mountain I could try to climb. "Trust is Weakness". I built every aspect of my life around this mantra. Do not trust anyone, anything, at anytime, because trust was always a lie. If you ever trust anything in life the only result you will get is pain. Everyone always leaves in the end, no matter how much they act like they care. The truth is they only care about using your affection to get what they need, and then leave you. Slowly and methodically, my mind began to shut down during this period. I stopped caring more and more until I got to the point where I felt no emotions whatsoever. I felt nothing, neither good nor bad. That way it eliminated all chance of getting hurt. You can't be hurt emotionally if you have no feelings to hurt in the first place. The only downfall of this is this is the definition of the word "sociopath".

CHAPTER FIVE: THE HYPOCRITE REVELATION

If there was a straw that broke the camel's back, it was what happened next. My mother kicked my stepfather out of the house. I had no idea why, and I truly didn't care. During this period I felt like my mom was actually nice for a change. We spent time with each other, and had time for a deep conversation one day. I probably should have never asked her, but I was curious why my dad got kicked out of the house. What she told me was absolutely shocking. The revelation of what really happened gave me this feeling of betrayal. He was a drug addict, and a lifelong member to the club, to be exact. He was addicted to heroin, and my mother had finally had enough of his nonsense and kicked him out of the house. This information sent shockwaves through my mind. I began to flashback to moments when we would be screaming in my dad's ear to get his attention, and he would just stay in this trance like state completely unresponsive. Time and time again, I remembered similar events like this taking place and suddenly a lot of things made sense about his behavior.

As my mind continued a journey through the past putting the pieces of the puzzle together, I suddenly realized one major thing about his actions towards me. What about the time he caught me doing drugs and his response to that incident? I remembered how low and insignificant I was made to feel by this very person for being a drug addict. Then I thought of all the awful treatment I had received from this self-righteous hypocrite for doing drugs. All the while, he was a bigger drug addict than I was. I thought back to how guilty I felt for letting my parents down. To try and say I was angry about this would be a complete understatement. I felt the purest form of hate any human could feel. All my other problems only compounded on top of this one. For the first time in my life, I felt completely justified that someone should die at my hands. My stepfather had earned the right by all his evil and hypocritical deeds that I should kill him. Society and human civilization would be better off if his life ended as soon as possible. That way he couldn't further ruin this world with his parasite-like, cancerous presence.

At that point I started to make plans as to how I would end his life. I knew when I carried this out I wouldn't hesitate a second or even feel an ounce of remorse. I realized deep down that these were not normal human responses that anyone should feel about everyday problems. You shouldn't be able to shrug off murdering someone like you were swatting a fly off a refrigerator door. The difference now is when I realized these feelings were wrong, I didn't care anymore. I liked the way I felt.

My mother admitted to me another shocking revelation during this period when my father was absent. She admitted the fact that she knew about the abuse that I suffered at the hands of my step father and did nothing to stop it. She was very grieved by this, and wept bitterly when she explained it to me. This sadly only fueled my rage even hotter towards my mother and humanity as a whole. I felt complete disdain for my mother and dropped all emotional attachment to her at that very moment. I was spinning out of control and rushing faster and faster towards a severe psychotic break. I would never believe anyone at the time if they would have told me just how deep into the abyss of suffering I would actually travel. God's long term plan was greater than the devils attempt to destroy me. Instead of being disintegrated into the fires of hell, I was actually to be refined by the eternal fire of God's love and grace. In the meantime, my thoughts began to turn only to violence, hate, and evil every waking moment.

On top of everything else, the impossible was about to happen. Once again, my mother shocks me by letting my step father move back into the house. All my negative emotions instantly boiled to the surface. The mere sight of either of them made me sick to my stomach. They were disgusting excuses for human beings, and I hated the thought of being in the same house as them. At the same time, the sheer stress of all my mental anguish was getting harder and harder for me to bear. My drug use got even worse during this period. Most other functions of life took a back seat to my getting high. I finally came to the point where all my only motivation was to get high. Anything else had almost no meaning in my life.

Shortly after my father's return to the house, something had to give. I moved out, staying with one of my closest friends for awhile just to get rid of those evil people. That living situation didn't last long because I had no real resources to take care of myself. A part of me thought maybe this time would be different living at home. Obviously it wasn't, nor would it ever be. Only a couple days after returning home, my dad tried to tell me what to do, and I absolutely blew a gasket. I put him down with everything I could think of that might hurt his feelings. I used every curse word invented by man at least fifty times each. To top off the entire scene, I issued a bold ultimatum to my mother that I knew I would win. I told her to choose right then and there between him and me. She could either have her flesh and blood, first born son in her life, or she could keep her drug addicted, abusive husband. To me, her response was almost guaranteed. Who wouldn't choose their child when given this choice? I told her either he leaves or I leave, because if I stay in the house with him even one more day, I will kill him. The choice she made was really the ultimate betrayal in my mind.

She told me, "I think you need to leave". This was the response given to my foolproof ultimatum. I had been denied by my own mother, and my hateful spew of obscenities shifted directions towards her. Any negative way of explaining how she was a bad mother came rolling out of my mouth. I made it clear how much I really hated her. I told her that every bad thing I had ever been through was her fault. What kind of psychopath lets someone beat her own children and does absolutely nothing to stop it? I told her she should just kill herself now and go straight to hell, where she was going anyway.

The way I am explaining it now actually puts a very light spin on how mean and vile my treatment was to my mother that day. By this point in my life, I had already beaten up my own mother and called her every nasty word in the dictionary. What a resume I was building up for myself. Believe it or not, these were considered good times in my life, because all the bad stuff was just about to happen.

CHAPTER SIX: INTO THE RABBIT HOLE

Hate, it is all I felt all the time. The demonic influences surrounding me were probably the strongest they've ever been at this point in my life. This would be the combination and climax of all the evil the devil had systematically placed within my heart. Separately, all the wrong that had happened to me throughout my life had been slowly brewing for years. Now this satanic meal would be served full strength all at once to my weak and mortal human soul.

The more drugs I did to numb the pain, the less and less they helped. If I didn't use drugs, however, I felt even worse. There had to be some kind of release from my psychological torment. It was too much to bear, and I got to the point where I would do anything to make it stop. As I was contemplating how in the world I would make this end, I kept coming to the same conclusion. There was only one way this torture would end, and I welcomed this option with open arms. I even grew to love this way of escape as my ultimate hope for freedom. It was a very simple and wonderful plan. I would just kill myself, and then my pain would end forever. I don't know why I didn't think of this before. That's all I wanted was for the pain to stop, and this would finally give me the rest that I had thirsted for my entire life.

The first major case of me trying to end my life was supposed to be a top secret plan. This way, even if someone did find out about my intentions, there was no way they would ever find me. It was very obvious that I was visibly distraught that evening to anyone around me. I asked a friend to give me a ride home and then promised her I would go straight to bed, to sleep off my depression. Before she left, I gave her all the money I had in my pockets, and told her it was a gift or some story like that. The truth was I knew I wouldn't need the money anymore. You can't spend money when you're dead. I waited about twenty minutes. Then I jumped in my car and started to drive. I hit the freeway out of town and just continued driving. I drove and drove, and ended up at this cheap motel in the middle of nowhere, in a town that I had no idea what the name was. Nobody would find me here because even I didn't know where I was.

I paid for the room, even though I wasn't old enough to rent a motel room. The owner just appreciated my money and rented me the room, no questions asked. Once inside my final resting place, I cried for hours at the torment that was my life. The pain and misery I felt was indescribable even to me now. All I wanted to do was sleep forever and never awake again to all this pain. I remember nothing but darkness engulfing every aspect of my soul. Razor blades, blood, and death was the itinerary for that night. Finally, I would have my peace. The next thing I realize, I wake up laid out in the middle of the floor, and to my despair I was still alive. The whole plan had failed, just like everything else in my life.

It wasn't even hard the first time I tried to kill myself. In fact, it wasn't hard any of the multiple times that I attempted to end my life. On the contrary, it felt natural and right in every way possible. There was one problem however, and that was for some reason, I couldn't die. Truthfully, no matter what I did, I could not kill myself. Razor blades, pills, and alcohol, and every time I would magically come back. I was even a failure at suicide, I thought to myself. I couldn't figure out why I wouldn't die. It was as if some supernatural force was in play, preventing it from happening. Even at the time I didn't really believe this to be true, but I did know that for some reason I could not die. I just assumed it was a continuing part of the curse that was my life. Even Death himself couldn't take away my pain.

On another occasion that I would choose to knock on deaths door, I knew I wouldn't make the same mistake twice. This time, I would grab the prize that I yearned for so dearly all these years. The only mistake I didn't make in my first suicide attempt was the location I picked to kill myself. This time it was on a late Friday night, and I picked the perfect place where nobody would think to look for me. I broke into a school, and that is where I would breathe my last wretched breath. No one would enter the school again for at least another two whole days. By then any hopes of reviving me would be a futile attempt. One thing I needed to change was my mode of execution. I chose the sure fire method of huge amounts of sleeping pills mixed with large amounts of alcohol. I ate an entire package of sleeping medication and drank until I fell asleep, hopefully forever. Both times I should have died easily. As before, the only result was mysteriously waking up the next morning perfectly safe, without a scratch.

After this second failure, some major questions started to pop into my head. None of this made any sense that I wasn't dead right now, and it was really bugging me that I was still breathing. Something else was involved here and I couldn't figure out what. This then raised my curiosity to find out just what was happening here. Time and time again I would seek to end my life, and the results were always the same. It was always hanging over my head that it didn't make sense that I wasn't dead.

Obviously some supernatural force was preventing me from killing myself. I realized this as a fact of life and had come to terms with accepting it. There was still a chance however, that somebody else could achieve this goal for me. I had made plenty of enemies in life so far, so there would be no shortage of volunteers for the job. The new plan would be very simple.

It consisted of getting a person who hated me enough to kill me. Not complicated in itself, but I had no idea how hard it really is to go against God's plans. Maybe I could finally have that which I have always wanted. Searching for death became an obsession for me. It got to the point that I sought her out every second of the day. Trying to kill myself was a very satisfying hobby.

How would I carry out these suicide missions? The simple explanation is I go around people who want to kill me, and that's exactly what they would do. More sad and in depth is the way I got them to want to kill me. My friends and I would get as high and drunk as possible every day to start. It wasn't just me that was certifiably insane. We all loved violence, and more specifically, the act of inflicting violence on other people. Day after day, night after night, we would savagely beat down innocent people for no other reason than our own personal amusement. We would all pack into our cars to drive in any random direction and just wait for the first person we saw walking down the street. Once we spotted our first victim, who was usually just minding their own business, we would give them the most savage and violent mugging possible. This was all to vent the pent up hate and disdain we felt for the world around us. The power, happiness, and peace that kicking somebody's face into the concrete would bring us, was better than any Christmas morning. As soon as we were done hospitalizing an innocent person, we quickly got back into our cars to drive to our next appointment on our schedule. It was always the same thing: finding another random person was just walking down the road, and then trying to top the first beating with an even more ruthless and savage attack. This is what we did, person after person, time and time again, night after night. After a couple years the number of people that we had given hospitalization beat downs was too high to even keep track of.

Sometimes we would self righteously justify these attacks by putting ourselves in the role of vigilantes. We would wait outside local pornography shops like a pack of wolves, waiting for the next pervert to walk into our waiting trap. Before we would try and break very bone in their face, we would ask them if they liked porn. This way their disgusting brains would know that what they were doing was an abomination. They could thank their sick, sexually deviant desires for the immense pain they were about to receive.

Doing this to a large number of the local population gives them the desire to wish you deceased. This is exactly what I was counting on in order to finish my ultimate plan of killing myself. The stage was set for me to only re-confront any one of these people, and then I would willingly accept the wrathful death sentence they would carry out. In my mind, the plan was foolproof, but once again, something else had other plans.

By myself, unarmed in any way, and unannounced to my friends, I would wander back into the very places and neighborhoods where all my enemies were known to frequent. I was hoping that by chance a bullet would find its way into my brain. I ventured into enemy territory, crossing my fingers that a knife would cut its way through one of my major arteries. Alas, I couldn't find the violent death that I so yearned for every waking moment of my life. Something would not let me die. When I realized this, at the same time I also knew it meant that I couldn't die. If I couldn't die, then I was going to take that out on every person who stepped in my way. Everyone would feel my bitterness for the curse I had been given. As a result, I continued on my violent lifestyle, hating everyone and everything associated with this world.

Soon after this is when I started to have blackouts and nervous breakdowns from reality. My brain couldn't handle the real world anymore so it began to retreat back into itself. When this first started to happen, I was really scared. One time all I was doing was giving my sister a ride somewhere in my car. When I went to pick her up, I had forgotten to turn my headlights off and the battery was completely drained of power. As I turned the key to start my car, all I heard was the click of the ignition switch. Most people wouldn't have a problem with this, and would continue on with their lives un-phased. Most people, even if this did bother them, would get pissed off and yell out some obscenitics. I wasn't most people, so I had quite a different reaction. I ran into the back yard bawling like it was the end of the world, and fell down, curled up in the fetal position on the dirt. If that wasn't bad enough, what was going on inside my head took it to a whole new level of weird. My mind literally shut down the entire outside world and retreated into itself. The only way to explain this to someone who hasn't experienced this phenomenon is to imagine a person driving on a long road trip. You have driven for so long that even though you want to continue driving, you are so tired that you just can't drive any longer. Then you hear a voice from the back seat that says, "Hey, why don't you let me take over for awhile and you can just rest"? "You can take over again when you feel better". This is exactly what started to happen with my mind. I was so tired mentally that I couldn't drive my life anymore. I couldn't drive so I let somebody else drive for me. When looking at this analogy in a figurative sense, it doesn't sound so bad. In reality, the definition of what was happening to me was a lot more tragic and sad. I couldn't handle the extreme stress of my life, so I created another personality who could. At first this sounded like a good thing.

The first time this happened, it lasted only a few minutes. Then it happened again, except this time it lasted about five minutes. It kept happening more and more frequently, with longer and longer intervals. During these periods, I would be aware that there was an outside world that continued to go on around me. The only thing is I had nothing to do with it because I wasn't a part of it. I had my own world that I belonged to inside my head. This world was a safe and peaceful place where I would never be hurt. This was a retreated haven where I was protected inside my own mind. At this point I didn't fully understand what was happening to me. I never really worried about that part of it and let myself enjoy the peacefulness of the experience. I remember that around my eighteenth birthday, I was in one of these nervous breakdown modes for over a week. I just sat there like an un-programmed robot. I was like a doll that nobody would play with, motionless for days at a time. Physically I was there, but I might as well have been 2000 miles away in a different country. I wasn't really living during this period of my life. I was a scared little kid hiding in his room under the bed until I was sure the boogeyman wasn't there anymore. In the meantime, I would just rest within myself. I rested from all the ugliness that I ran away from in the first place. It felt peaceful to know I could get away anytime I wanted to relax in my own personal tree house, atop the middle of my psyche. I had my own personal boy's club and I was the only member. I was the only member for now anyway. I bet if I could keep things that way I would have stayed inside my head forever and never came back out. Who needs the world anyway? Not me. All those other people out there who love it so much can keep it for themselves. I had my own little world that I created and all I wanted was to be left alone. I probably would have been alone forever in my head if I actually was the only person there.

I wasn't, however, and that meant I wasn't the only one with access to my personal social hall. This is the point when everything fell apart.

One night I was out burglarizing anything I could get my hands on. I got the bright idea, along with my friend, to steal the overnight cash boxes from the local snow-cone shacks in town. For a few seconds of work we would have 50 dollars for each place we robbed. Back then, any amount of money, no matter how small the amount, was worth breaking into a business. If you built up a big enough pile of money you could buy more drugs with it. Obviously buying and doing more drugs was the ultimate and only goal in my life at this time. After we had broken into about the seventh one, we noticed a cop car drive past us at a very slow speed. They were interested in what we were doing inside a business we didn't own at three o'clock in the morning. Long story short, they pulled us over and found out exactly what our night's entertainment was all about. Some handcuffs, a police car ride, and eight hours of the booking process later, I found myself arrested downtown. I hated my life, and to make it worse, everyone else was getting bailed out while I had to ride it out with the justice system. I got transferred to the county jail outside of town and stayed there for 2 ½ weeks. This is actually chump change as far as jail sentences go. It was my first time ever being locked up, so it was a completely miserable experience. Finally they realized I was just a small time crook and let me go on probation, to watch over myself. Essentially, I was put on the honor system, since I falsely told them I wouldn't do it again. At the time, I actually did mean the promise I gave them. It was mostly due to the fact that I was literally begging them to let me out of a human cage. The long term permanence of that promise was very short lived, since only four months later, I found myself back in that same cage.

Once again, I made a feeble effort to show up at a church service now and then, without any real expectations of changing my lifestyle. I guess I was hoping that by gracing God's church with my presence I would appease his wrath away from my hypocritical intentions. I continued partying, being a violent psychopath, was still a drug addict, and was an overall refuse of a human being until the night my life changed forever.

At the time I was staying with a friend, and I came home one night at two in the morning from a night of partying. Immediately upon entering the residence, I was informed that I needed to move out the next day, because I wasn't welcome in the house anymore. For some reason, this was the most discouraging news I had gotten up until this time since I had no other options on the table. I ran into my room, bawling like a little girl, inconsolably. In the fetal position, rocking back and forth, I kept saying, "help me, help me, help me" over and over to the lifeless walls of my lonely room. I was very surprised to next hear a response to my desperate call from the bottom of my soul. (Excuse the foul language in the following quotes, but I wanted the realness of this moment to be brought across exactly as it happened)

"Shut up, shut the f*ck up, look how pathetic you are!"

I looked up to see who was responding to me when I heard the voice again.

"You think your friends will help, you think anyone will help you? Nobody will help you! Nobody is there for you, and nobody ever will be there for you. I'm the only one who has ever been there for you!"

Looking around, I realized there was nobody else in the room with me. The terror of this fact brought a complete panic over my entire being. Sweating, I ran to my mirror to look at the pathetic shell I had become, and tried to pull myself together. That's when I heard the ghost of a voice speaking to me once again. This time I realized another and even more frightening piece to this insane puzzle. This invisible voice that spoke out of thin air was actually coming from my own lips. Gazing into the mirror, I saw that I was speaking to myself somehow without realizing it. How can this happen you ask? Well, I was asking myself the same question at that very moment.

I was absolutely petrified with fear. For some reason I immediately started to pray. I don't even know what I was hoping to accomplish with this task. I guess I wasn't sure if I had been visited by a demon or if I was possessed by one. Either way, I knew this wasn't right, and I didn't want it happening to me. Then just as mysteriously as it had appeared, all of a sudden the other entity was gone. Completely stunned and shocked, I was left speechless sitting on my bed. It was as if time had stood still and the life I once knew would never be the same again. After this moment all I remember is crying myself to sleep.

The next day started exactly where the last one ended, with me being completely speechless. It went on that way for at least three days as I tried to wrap my head around what really happened. There was a part of me that understood what happened since I was there. The logical side of my brain kept dismissing it as fiction because stuff like that isn't real. After all I understand that you kill a werewolf with a silver bullet to the heart, but that doesn't make monsters real. Why? Because monsters aren't real, are they? Once upon a time I had believed this fairy tale. Now my eyes were opened to the truth. Monsters were real and I think I was becoming one of them.

CHAPTER SEVEN: DIVINE APPOINTMENT

I remember the day that changed the rest of my life in a bitter sweet fashion. A part of me hates that day due to the atrocity committed by my own hands. Yet there is another part of me that recognizes this day was the first step onto my path of redemption. I had just gotten off work, and was about to go home for the day. For some reason I hung around an extra ten minutes to skateboard in the parking lot which I had never done before, because I hated to work and always wanted to go directly home. Today was different in many other ways as I would come to find out. As I was driving home and pulling onto the street where I lived, I noticed somebody on a bicycle riding in the middle of the road. Being the constant ball of anger that made up my daily life, of course this pissed me off because I wanted to go home. Naturally I start yelling curse words at this person. Not only was he in my, way but he wouldn't get out of my way even though he knew I needed to pass. Eventually he moved to the side and I think nothing else of the whole experience. I arrived in my driveway and opened my door and started to gather my work belongings when something really surprised me.

I felt a very distinct sting in my jaw all of a sudden. I have known this feeling before, but was confused as to why I felt it at this moment. I was being sucker punched in the jaw, which is normally where you hit someone when trying to knock them out. However, I was suffering from a constant psychotic rage that left my entire body numb to most external pain all together, so this did nothing more than to get my attention. My attacker continued an attempt to assault me, and further wanted to continue the attack by pulling me out of my car. What he saw was a young teenager who was going to be an easy target to beat up and rob. I found out later through many people who knew this individual that his M.O. was to jump and rob defenseless people in order to obtain money for drugs. He also had a notorious reputation for being a tough guy, who was in and out of prison his whole life. His cause was to be furthered upon myself, who at a first glance seemed to be a more than easy target to his shenanigan lifestyle. Yet this was a case of a very mean and nasty convict who loved to fight against a homicidal psychopath with multiple personalities whose hobby was to mug people for fun. This equation was destined to equal something very bad and tragic.

As I was being dragged out of my car, I grabbed one of the many weapons I had laying around for these types of situations that I always seemed to be in. This time it was a baseball bat that I kept right next to my driver's seat. He had no clue what he was dragging out of the car along with me, but he would soon find out. I struck him in the ribs as hard as I could with the baseball bat to try and get him off of me. It only backed him up for a couple seconds; then again he lunged forward to continue the assault. Again I slammed the bat into his body as hard as I could to try and get him to stop. Once again, he only stepped back for a second or two. The last time, I swung so hard I tried to swing all the way through him, and this was what made him finally concede to stop. The confrontation was far from over however, because he then realized he could not get the best of me. At this moment, it was abundantly clear that he would return to exact his revenge on me. He told me he would kill me the next time he saw me and that only he would know when that was. I tried to end the whole situation by attempting to shake hands, but after a few seconds of contemplative thought, he would have nothing of it. He had made up his mind that he would come back in a moment of surprise and end my life.

This decision, of course, was not acceptable in any way, shape, or form in my mind. What if he tried to kill me around my family and they got hurt? Mostly, I was just enraged that he had not learned that you do not mess with me. Hadn't he figured out what was going to happen to him when he threatened me? As he rode away on his bike, I followed him in my car to hopefully end this whole situation with a bloody fist fight and then I would use my jiu jitsu to end all hope of ever getting the best of me. As soon as I saw him, he started to try to pull me out of my car again, trying to once again sucker punch me into a vulnerable position. I simply got back into my car, ran him over, and drove away.

My first emotion was the shock of how naturally it came to me. The next thing I felt was a sense to run and never stop to let all this catch up to me. That's what I attempted to do-run away. Just like Jonah trying to run to the other side of the world, this was all a futile attempt to hide from God. He had me on his radar far before this happened, and I couldn't run from him any longer. My day of reckoning had come from the creator to gather up his creation. I had screwed my life up far enough, and he needed to take over in a very direct way. I had the idea that I would run for the rest of my life, never finding rest, and forever looking over my shoulder for the authorities who were chasing me for all the atrocities in my lifetime. At the time, it seemed like a good and feasible plan. It was better than any other alternative I could come up with at the moment. Out of fear, I turned to the last person I would ever turn to for help-my biological father. In fact, that was the reason I turned to him for help. If he was the last person I would turn to for help, than he would be the last person the cops would think I was with, which would give me a big head start. I called him on the phone, pleading for his help and for any ideas as to what I should do at this point. His whole life he had been a criminal, so if anyone would know what to do, it would be him. His first advice was to get out of town immediately, which I agreed was a good idea. I would drive up to Oregon where he lived, and for the mean time lay low for awhile. Once I was there, we would figure out what my long term plans were to be. I honestly thought that the more time passed, eventually, this would just go away and be forgotten. My mind was panicking and it just wanted to see a ray of hope at the end of the tunnel. The brightest light that ever existed was waiting at the end of the tunnel, but not the one I was thinking of going through. As fast as I could I went to one of my friends house's and made her give me ride to get some clothes and supplies so that I wouldn't be using my car out on the streets. One by one, I started calling all the people who I considered to be my friends, telling them that I would be going away for awhile, but to not worry about me because I would be safe and okay. I spent the night crying and in disbelief that my life had gotten to this point. The whole situation was like one big dream that I couldn't wake up from, no matter how hard I tried or wished to.

Trying to run, I quit my job, gathered up my clothes and essential belongings, and made an attempt to drive to Oregon to stay with my father. Nobody would know to look for me there. I said my goodbyes to all the people who needed to hear them and the next day I set out on the road. A constant paranoid feeling had engulfed my psyche. Would anyone ever find out where I was? Would I be on the run for the rest of my life? Would I ever have a normal life living like this? What now? I would get a job, I thought, and when the heat died down, eventually I could probably come back to visit my family and friends. I could get myself settled in Oregon and my life would be okay for once. Maybe this was the best thing that ever happened to me since it will finally give me the reason to do something with my life. My brain was still searching for a happy ending to this whole story. I would get my life together and when I did finally return, I would do so as the conquering hero who everyone knew would eventually have the whole world in his hands. It would be a great and glorious day when all my adoring friends who missed their leader so much would finally be graced by my presence once again. My ego and vanity were out of control, even in this direst of situations. I knew that I was better and smarter than everyone else, so I would find a way out of this and end up on top like I always did before. I had to be alright I thought to myself, because that is what I do. In the end I always come out on top… so I tricked myself into believing.

I temporarily interrupted this train of thought by stopping into a rest stop to go to the bathroom. When I went back to my car, I turned the ignition to find that my car wouldn't start. Again and again, I tried in vain to start my old automobile which I had not taken care of in any sense of the word. I actually attempted to pray that God would start the car for me. Can you believe the audacity in that whole prayer? It was probably God himself who let the car break down, and I'm praying against his will to let me continue running from my actions. But you can't go against the will of God, no matter how hard you try, and he had me exactly where he wanted me. For ten hours I waited at that rest stop for my uncle to come and pick me up, only to take me right back to the place I was trying to run from in the first place. It was like swimming up a river through a bunch of rapids. I could run from the consequences of my actions and my heavenly Father no longer. So much anger was coursing through my veins but I was forced to sit there and contemplate the reaping of all the evil crops that I had sewn up to that point. I was stuck ten hours in the middle of nowhere, all alone with nothing but my thoughts. For me this was the worst possible situation I could ever imagine myself in; having to be alone with my thoughts and face the person I really was. I had no drugs to numb the pain and I had nowhere to go to preoccupy my sanity. There was no person whom I could focus on so that I didn't have to focus on myself. It was an absolutely horrible place for me to be in. God needed me to sit and really think about what I had done and what it is I was attempting to do. I had to remember all the people I had hurt over the years, especially my own family. The horrible things I had said and done to my parents hit me like a ton of bricks. All the people who ever cared about me with all their heart and soul, only for me to spit in their face time and time again with my complete lack of empathy toward the human race. I was probably the most selfish person in my own little world, and nobody else mattered except me and what I wanted. Anyone else who had opinions and feelings were always secondary to my aspirations and dreams for momentary pleasure. Finally, my uncle arrived at the rest stop, temporarily ending my own self torment, to give me a ride back to the scene of the crime which I was determined to sweep under the rug. The time spent at the rest stop actually gave me something to think about and forced me to rearrange my whole plan to leave town and running forever. I traded that crazy plan for an even more egotistical and absolutely insane plan.

My new plans where to stay in town and try and lay low, under the radar, until the heat died down. I let my close friends know about the new plans so that I could get their help when I needed it. I would not leave town and would just live my life as if nothing happened and all would be fine. I told my friends where I would be staying, and went about my business as usual. Business was anything but usual, however, because someone at the house read the morning newspaper and noticed a very unusual headline that day. There was a very violent hit and run that had happened, and the police were exhausting every avenue possible to catch whoever was responsible for this horrible crime. If anyone had any information concerning this case, in the name of justice, they were to contact the detectives investigating the crime. I wasn't worried because nobody knew I did it except some of my closest friends, and they would never do anything like rat on me. I was too important and great for them to do that. Now, I could brag about this to everyone, and they could think I was even tougher than before. My legend was growing greater by the second. I went back by my house to take a shower. My uncle knocked on the bathroom door to inform me that the police where there to arrest me. How do they even know that I am here? I thought about running, but I was naked and it was the end of November. I got dressed in my finest clothes and was placed in handcuffs as I got into the back of the police cruiser. All I could hear was my family telling me over and over to ask for a lawyer and to not tell them a thing. A part of me wanted to explain my side of the story, but I did what my family asked of me and immediately asked for a lawyer when I got down to the police station.

Not talking made the detectives very unhappy and I was soon arrested for hit and run. They booked me into the jail, which I still remembered very vividly from my last stay there. It was just as unpleasant the second time as it was the first. The jail had the same awful food, along with the same rude guards. I knew that this was all a big misunderstanding, and as soon as I talked with my lawyer, he would let me tell the detectives my side of the story. I figured I would let them know this was all an accident, and that he attacked me first so that whole situation was a case of self defense. Once they got all the information straight, I would be let out and free to go in a couple days at the most. Even if it took a couple of weeks like my last stay in jail, I would definitely be home for Christmas, bragging to all my friends about how I had once again evaded death's sting and escaped the law as I had always done before. This would all get straightened out in a couple of days, and then I could get back to living my life as I had before. These were my plans… God's plans were very different and would take me literally in the opposite direction.

CHAPTER EIGHT: JUDGE, JURY, & EXECUTIONER

Being arrested is a long, tedious, and annoying process. All together, it usually takes about 8-10 hours to go through the entire booking scenario. You do a little paper work and then wait for 2 hours. Then you take a few pictures and then wait another 3 hours. After that, you answer a few questions and you wait 5 hours for them to give you your clothing and eventually put you inside of a cell with other people. Honestly, by the time the whole process is complete, you are so emotionally and physically exhausted you just go straight to sleep once you get in your bunk. If you want, you can make your one phone call to tell your family that you're okay, or cry to them to bail you out. Or you can skip calling your family and call the local bail bond company to come get you. I forget now what the first amount was that I needed to bail out. I figured I didn't need to go through all that since they would be letting me go in a couple of days anyway, once they found out what really happened. Then something happened that caused me to start worrying, just a little bit.

A friend of mine, who was my best friend at the time, came to visit me in the downtown lockup. When someone visits you, it is not a face to face encounter. You are behind glass and all communication is conducted through a phone line. Now this phone is tapped with a microphone which records your every word. This is intentional, so that if you say anything to a loved one that will incriminate you or reveal your guilt in a particular crime, they can use this evidence against you. I was very aware of this fact, and was very reluctant to reveal any information about the alleged incident that I was involved in. This friend (who I came to find out later was the one who turned me into the police in the first place) was only interested in a certain topic on that particular day. She wanted to know what exactly happened the day of the crime. Time and time again, she wanted to know the truth, but just as many times, I explained that I could not talk about it over these recorded phone calls. Finally, she gave up, and we were about to end the call, but she pulled out her cell phone and called the lead detective in the case, right in front of me. She told the detective that she could not get me to talk, and what should they do next? At this time, I was escorted back to my cell to deeply contemplate what it was that really just took place. Finally, I realized that I was being set up by one of the closest friends I had ever had. I realized a lot of things at that point. I was in a lot of trouble, and every bit of it was my fault. I now knew my friends were not really my friends. I was finally coming to the truth about my situation that I found myself involved with: there was a good chance that I was going to jail for a really long time.

A couple of days later was Thanksgiving, so I decided to call my grandmother and see how she was faring with me being locked up. During this phone call I realized even deeper that my fate was now completely out of my hands. My grandma gave me the absolutely devastating news that the man I had run over had passed away earlier that day. My first thought was how sad it was to die on Thanksgiving. Then I thought about how his family could never again enjoy a Thanksgiving holiday for the rest of their lives. Next, only one thought ran through my mind, over and over, until I was literally sick to my stomach. I had killed another human being. I was a murderer. This wasn't a dream and I definitely was not waking up from this situation.

66

The following days were the most lonely and depressing of my entire life. I had no friends, no family, and now I was being charged with first degree murder. They told me there was also a chance that they would seek the death penalty in my case. This was due to the special circumstances in the crime. At first I thought this was actually a good thing, as I thought they would let me go when they figured out the special circumstances surrounding the case. If you ever find yourself being arrested, God forbid, and they say your case has special circumstances. This is the worst thing that can be said. It means usually only one thing, and that is that the district attorney is seeking the death penalty in the case. As things went from bad to worse, I was really starting to feel the stress of the whole situation. I didn't want to be alone in this situation, but I found myself nowhere but alone. Long ago, most of my immediate family had left me to my own consequences. The few friends that I thought I had were setting me up with the same police detectives who were trying to put me on death row. This was the culmination of how my life ended up when I was in charge. When I was left to run my own life, this is the result of the evil that I had planted in my world. I was alone with nothing, and the only thing left to show for it was a trip to the death chamber. How had things gotten to such low a point in my life? Asking myself this question brought only a sarcastic chuckle from my lips that only the most pathetic of cases could laugh at. Right around this time, I got a glimmer of hope in a letter one lonely night.

The letter was actually written by my father, on behalf of my mother. We were so far apart that she was afraid to even write to me herself. She had asked him to write to me to see if it was okay to come and visit. She wanted to know if we could try and start over. Not to pretend that nothing bad had ever happened between us, but that we should just start over. I, for one, was all for this invitation to a treaty for peace, even if was on a temporary basis. I needed someone to reach out to me because this was the loneliest I had ever felt in my entire life. I just needed somebody, anybody, even if that person was my worst enemy. In this case it was a literal example of my worst enemy being the only person who really reached out for me in my darkest hour. She came to visit me soon after, and I admit I still held a lot of animosity towards her for all the pain that I felt she caused me in life.

Although at the moment, it was more important to me that she was just there. The fact that she was still acknowledging me as being a person was one of the nicest gestures that had ever been extended to me in this life. It had a big enough impact on me that I started to contemplate my whole life in general. I wanted something different than all the pain and suffering that I was used to. It had grown old, feeling nothing but hate every waking second of the day. I now knew that the only result that could ever come of a life like that was my current situation. I decided to give my mother another chance. I also decided to give another person the first chance that he had been asking me for my whole life. I finally said yes to God and for the only time up until then, I was ready to let him take 100% control of the situation. I wanted to turn my life completely over to his will and let him drive the rest of the way. I was done driving my own life, and all of it had made me very tired physically and mentally exhausted.

The next development in my story was definitely an immediate spiritual attack brought on by Satan for my recent spiritual conversion. I was informed by many sources close to me (and some not so close) that there were a lot of people who wanted to avenge the death of a certain individual that I had recently come in contact with. There were a lot of people very unhappy at me for what I had done to receive my current criminal charges. At this point in my life, I was given a great conundrum of a puzzle to figure out. I was a killer but did not want to be anymore. Many people were probably going to come after me trying to kill me. If that happened, there would only be two choices as to the outcome: I either kill or be killed. Despite my recent change in life philosophy, I knew I had absolutely no problem killing anybody who got in my way. This, however, was not an outcome that I wanted played out again in my lifetime, so I needed an alternative solution to this problem. I chose a scenario that would get me out of having to end someone's life, and at the same time prove to myself and God that I really wanted to change. I chose to go into protective custody and live the rest of my prison life by myself, as an outcast who had publically given up the life of violence in the other prisoner's eyes. I was moved to another unit where I was immediately invited to church by the first person that I met. I took it as a sign from God that he approved of my trivial self sacrifice in trying to better my life. For once in as long as I can even remember, I felt like I had done the right thing. It was the first step on a very long road to redemption for me.

I have to tell you that even though I was going through the circumstances that I was, this was one of the happiest times of my life. All the different people on the unit would hold a church service in one of the cells every morning, and also in the afternoon. Depending on who was in the unit, we would have on average anywhere from 10 to 18 people in attendance. For whatever reason they were there, we all would have one thing in common during the service, and that was freedom. In a cliché way our bodies were locked up but our souls were free. None of the guards could take that away from us and neither could our pasts. For that reason, it was one of the happiest times of my life. No matter what was happening to us in the courts, we knew that we had God on our side so it was like the ultimate ace up our sleeves. I knew that with God stepping up to bat for me, nobody could stand in my way. I finally started to recognize that God had been tugging on my heart for a very long time. It wasn't just to start going to church either, but for a bigger purpose than run-of-the-mill Christianity as I understood it. He was calling me to call other people to him. I think deep down I always knew this to be a fact, but it had never lined before with my agenda. Maybe this was the whole reason I got arrested in the first place-to finally accept my calling to ministry. I was right about this, but definitely not in the way I expected it to turn out. I thought I would be released from jail and then I would go on to do work in a church somewhere, telling people about my horror tale of spending months in county jail.

Every time I went to court, I knew that this would be the time God intervened and the judge would let me go. Then the first court trip left me back in the same place I was before. My response was to go back to the church services on the unit and praise God even louder than before. I knew he was on my side, so I had nothing to worry about. Besides, all the people in the Bible had a testing of their faith now and then, so why would I be any different? My next trip to court yielded the same results as before. I was empty handed inside of a cell at the end of the day. After about the fifth trip, they started to talk about offering me a deal to take instead of going through a first degree murder trial. That's when I knew my time had come. Since the public needed some punishment in the case, they had to keep me in jail for a little while. Ultimately, they knew the time would come where they would have to let me go based on the evidence in my favor. Better to let me go having served a few months in jail than let me go without serving any time at all. Someone needed to be punished for justice's sake, and that is what these last few months were all about. Now, though, my time had come for this great wrong to be rectified, and I should be let go with my time served in the eyes of the law.

At the court house I was shocked and amazed to learn that I was not going home that day. Further, the deal that they offered me was 18 years on one count of 2nd degree murder, and an additional 4-6 years for hit and run. The best deal they could offer me was at least 22 years in prison, and that is the soonest I could expect to be out. I have to tell you, the actual reality of the situation hadn't hit me until that moment. This was real, and I was possibly facing the rest of my life behind bars. It absolutely took the breath out of my lungs. I couldn't in my right mind agree to that deal, so I said no, expecting them to counter-offer me with less time. This was not the local swap meet however, and their rebuttal deal was that we will be starting your first degree murder trial tomorrow. At the beginning of the day, I was singing praise songs because God was so good for letting me go that day. When the day was over, I was absolutely in shock to be starting a trial for my very life the next day. There was no time to sit and feel sorry for myself as my lawyer and I put the finishing touches on the story that I would bring across as my defense. The truth wouldn't suffice since I was red handed guilty. Therefore, we needed to comb through the truth with a fine toothed comb, to weed out the facts that would send me to the death chamber. If there was one thing I knew I could do well, it was to lie with a straight face. After all, I was a sociopath who had no real feelings. The ones I did have, I would ship off to one of the three personalities that I had created as the ultimate self defense mechanism. The prosecutor would try and push my buttons to erupt emotions of anger in front of the jury to show them who I really was. The only problem was I had no emotions to push, so there would be no cat and mouse game to play on my part.

How quickly my morals went out the door. How fast I forgot the false conversion to Christianity. I was the worst example of a hypocrite, living an absolutely evil life while hiding under a fake veil of self-righteousness. I had only called on God because I needed his help to go free. I was caught in the act and I wanted his divine favor so he could stamp my "get out of jail free" card. I wasn't repentant of my sins, wanting to change my life for good. I was just sorry that I had got caught, and I didn't want to take responsibility for the crime that I had committed. I was a fraud, and the worst part is that after telling the lie so many times that I was innocent, I actually believed that I was.

I can name three times in my life when I was actually afraid. The first time was when my sister overdosed on New Year's during the Y2K scare. Another time was when my daughter got sick from sepsis and almost died. Then there was the time I started my trial for first degree murder. The whole scene, and how I felt, is almost indescribable with words or language. One second I am standing there being asked one last time if I want to accept the plea deal for 22 years, and then literally the next minute over one hundred possible jurors are filing into the courtroom. Both lawyers started to ask the jurors if they thought I was guilty before they heard the evidence. Most of the people thought I was guilty, just from hearing in the news what had taken place. I almost thought of asking for a change of venue (where we held the trial) because I wouldn't get a fair trial in my home town. Part of them were answering that way due to the fact that they wanted to excused from jury duty, but a big part of them really felt that way about my innocence. My life is on the line, and the people who hold that decision in their hands already don't believe I am innocent before hearing any of the evidence. This was a very disheartening feeling, and the reason this time was one of only three days in my life in which I was truly afraid.

After the three day process of selecting a jury was over, we then began the opening arguments. I have to say that people have said some bad things about me in my life, but this trial took the cake. Monster, maniac, murderer, killer, and pretty much every negative word in the dictionary were being directed toward my personal character. Both sides fought tenaciously to show what type of person I really was. One side was trying to build my character up, while the other was trying to tear me down. In an unbiased view, I would say they both did a surprisingly good job. I guess that is why they went to law school in the first place-to be good at their job. For a whole week, my friends and family were called onto the stand to either prove or disprove that I was a good person in life. There were many more cases of me being a bad person then examples of me doing good things. I really didn't like what the prosecutors were trying to do to me, but I couldn't help but respect their ruthless attitude toward the whole process. I was so engulfed by evil that I respected people who had the audacity to try and destroy me. This was my most respected characteristic in other human beings: the desire to destroy other people's lives and smile while they do it. Seeing that we were not making any headway in my defense, the whole trial rested on my own testimony.

The day before I testified, my lawyer visited me in jail to go over the last minute preparations in my story. He went over all the ways that the defense would try and make me snap out of character. He went over the weak points in our story and just made sure I was prepared for every possibility that could be thrown at me. When asked if I was ready to do this, my response was "No, but I have to be". As I took the stand, I was nervous about how important this situation was to my life in general. First up was my lawyer, which went really smoothly except for constant objections from the other side. Then the real pressure cooker began when the prosecution was up to bat. Time after time, they attempted to stir up my famous temper by pushing every last nerve I had in my body. I took the opportunity to look very young and innocent, with lots of tears to boot. Despite every instinct I had to do so, I never lost my temper and, all in all, actually came out on top in the situation. Now I just had to wait through the short final arguments and my life was in the jury's hands.

For another two days, I waited with sweaty palms and an upset stomach to see what my fate was going to be. The bailiff did me the very kind favor of letting me know periodical updates on which way the jury was leaning. Some of the news was bad and some was good, but none of it was definite yet the decision I really wanted to hear. Then I got word that they had made a final verdict in the case. The walk back to the courtroom took an eternity in my head. My entire family was present for this verdict reading and I couldn't help but wonder how this would affect them and what they would do without me for so long. As they read aloud that I was not guilty of first degree or second degree murder, I could see the look of gratefulness in my loved ones eyes. Then, right before they spoke the bad news, I mouthed the words to my sister that I loved her. I was found guilty of voluntary manslaughter and one count of hit and run. I would serve anywhere from four years and up to the possibility of even 15 years in prison. One thing was a fact-at that moment I was going to prison for a long, long time. This wasn't a dream and I wasn't waking up to live happily ever after.

I couldn't even speak to anyone back at the jail. I was absolutely stunned as to what had just taken place that day. I had been telling everyone to trust in God because he could deliver you like he was going to deliver me from the bondage of this prison cell. Now he hadn't delivered me at all, and I was going to be here a lot longer than most of the other people combined. Had God lost? In my eyes yes, but my thoughts are not those of God's. My wants and needs had selfish ambition behind them while God's plan was much bigger and righteous than my own. Eventually I would come to realize this fact, but sadly it wouldn't be anytime soon.

All this attention of me going back and forth to court was documented by the news media, bringing up some old baggage that I hoped was gone forever. You can't run from your past, because eventually you get tired and it catches up to you. People still wanted me dead over my crime and being on the news made me stick out like a sore thumb. One day a group of people had a meeting to decide my fate. I had to be punished and now was my reckoning. Different groups of people voted to see who was going to stab me, or just end my life in other creative ways. Once it was decided who would carry out the act, politics noted that nobody else could then seek vengeance or suffer the same fate as I did. Little did I know that the group who was seeking the most violence in the other's eyes secretly knew me, and were friends who did not want to see me get hurt. They convinced everyone else they were the men for the job, and got voted to have a green light on my life. They rushed me from behind and closed the cell door behind them, only to pretend to beat me up while they let me in on their plan. I had no idea that any of this had transpired, and was shocked to hear all the details. The sentence had been laid down upon my life and carried out. God had an obvious hand in all these undertakings, and an obvious miracle from heaven had saved my life. Only looking back on it now do I realize how amazing this all actually was. I haven't been able to fully appreciate God's love that day until now.

That whole circus was short lived as I once again focused my attention to my sentencing date. I kept running through all the scenarios in my head every second of the day. My best case option was that I get six years for the manslaughter starting out. Then, minus the year that I had already been in jail it would knock that down to five years. Also, with good behavior I could hope to be out in another two and a half years. This made the whole situation bearable to my mind, since that really is not too terribly long to be away from the world. For a month before the sentencing, I kept pep talking myself that this would be my fate. So much so that I believed that there would be no other option because God had willed it. I was actually now using manifest destiny to conquer the old west in my life all over again. When the day came to hear my fate for the next two years, I was once again very confident that things were going to go my way. What I didn't know is that I was once again about to eat some humble pie.

In court my normal prosecutor didn't even show up to plead against me. Instead, it was an upstart young lady who was a pit bull in the courtroom. Let me tell you, she was good at her job. My side had written letters to the judge, but so had the families of the victims. Both sides also had people testify on their behalf. I also wrote what I thought was a cry straight from my soul pleading for mercy from the judge who had my life in his hands. I figured my letter telling of how I changed my life and renounced my past for Christianity was a fool proof way of earning the shortest sentence possible. My efforts were turned upside down by the statements of the prosecutor, who said something that even to this day rips at my soul with truth. She mentioned that in my letter I was asking for mercy from the court for my crime. She said the only problem was that when given, mercy was something that is not deserved. God may give undeserved forgiveness, but the court of law doesn't give out things that are undeserved. Mr. Schutte deserves to be handed down justice and does not deserve to be given mercy for the horrible things that he has done. With that the judge sentenced me to eleven years in prison, and I all but gave up on the God who had allowed this to happen.

CHAPTER NINE: ARKHAM ASYLUM

This was all God's fault. If he actually was in control of this world as he claimed to be, then why was my entire life one big living hell since my childhood? How was I expected to turn out with everything that I was handed? All I was shown my entire life was violence, so that is all I knew. Why didn't God intervene and stop all the things that turned me into the monster I had become? Why did I have to raise my kid sister when I was a child myself? It wasn't fair that all I knew was this life of crime and now I was the one who was being punished for turning out the way I did. Did anyone expect any other ending than this outcome? Life was one big joke and so was the court system. It isn't about guilt or innocence, but more about how can the courts earn more money by sending as many people to prison as they can. God didn't have my best intentions in mind. Only one person has ever had my best intentions as his one goal. He was my best and only friend who has always wanted well for me. The only person that has looked out for me was me, and I turned back to the only friend that I ever truly had.

I really didn't know what to do next. How was I supposed to prepare for what I was facing in the future? My natural reaction was obviously to go into survival mode. I just really didn't know what that meant in this situation. All I really knew about prison was what I saw in movies, and that wasn't too pleasant. On top of that, I already had people who were looking to kill me. When would I once again face the backlash for my crime? Would I survive for the next eleven years? Why was this real? Why was this my life? Why?

About a month later, I got the call at 4:00am to get on the bus to prison. My heart wasn't beating fast, but I was anything but calm. Before I would go to my permanent prison home I had to spend a few months in a reception center. This is where they go over all your personal and case information to see which prison is best suited for you to spend your time. You go through a gambit of physical and mental testing, all to gauge how violent you are, or even to see if there is a glimmer of hope in your future. Those with severe physical problems like having AIDS or being paralyzed are all sent to different medical centers. People with mental illness are sent to places with psychiatric programs. Those who are involved in organized crime, and even police officers who have gone bad, all have a certain place where they are to spend their prison time. The reception center is where I first stopped on my long journey through prison life. By word of mouth, I heard these places were not as violent as most prisons. This wasn't true, because as soon as I got to this place I witnessed a very savage attack on another human being. I thought to myself, this is my life now, so it was time to get used to it. My new state of mind was eat or be eaten, kill or be killed, and nothing about this was figurative. To survive I needed to become that which I vowed to never become again. I needed to break a promise I made to God, but he wouldn't care since he doesn't care what happens to anybody anyway. The choice was a no-brainer what I had to do. Once again I was to turn back into a sociopathic, homicidal killer. Besides, maybe I could get some revenge for all the wrong that was done to me in the past year.

Needless to say, my thoughts were all over the place at this time in my life. With all the chaos going on in my head, there was only one consistent theme throughout it all, which was continuing to blame everybody else for my life. Deep down somewhere I knew all this was my fault, but I wasn't ready to face that kind of guilt. My approach was to do as I had always done-shift my thoughts somewhere other than myself. Then again, my lifelong attitude of doing this was getting me nowhere fast, so maybe it was time for a change. During my time in reception I was almost catatonic with shock about spending forever in prison. I was almost like a statue on a daily basis from paralyzing depression. I could barely eat or speak, let alone function as a human being. All this was being noted by the psychologists and psychiatrists, who further investigated the cause of my behavior. I started to open up to them about my past, and the events which led me to my current situation. They were particularly interested in the mental illness aspects to my fall in society. At that time I hadn't told too many people about this part of my life, so it was very hard to admit such weakness. That is what I thought about having these disorders: they were a weakness for not being tough enough to handle my environment growing up. The deeper they dug into my psyche, the more they realized how far off the radar I had really gotten. This earned me a ticket to a prison which also offered a psychiatric program to help prisoners deal with their mental health issues. I had never been a part of anything like this other than seeing a therapist. They also wanted to try placing me on medication to try and calm my tendencies toward violence. At first I didn't want to have any part of it, but I realized there were a lot of upsides to this, so I gave the whole plan a chance. Besides, maybe they would place me in a less violent place which will up my chances for survival.

One good thing about finally making it to prison was that I had free access to cigarettes. Believe me, after all the stress I had been through I needed to relax. Now I didn't smoke before I went to jail, but I did after going through a first degree murder trial. That type of stress is on a whole different level all of its own. Another good thing was even though prison food was awful; it tasted 2,000,000% better then county jail food. Prison food is sometimes made with the same bi-products used in dog food, but compared to county food I was in heaven. I came to find a lot of people in prison were actually nice people, other than being the most racist group of humans on earth. All in all, I was sadly adapting to my new super-violent environment a lot quicker than I expected. This fast transition was actually a bad thing, because no person should get used to a social setting such as that one. Everything that you see in movies that is bad about prisons is real. They don't sit around and make that stuff up because prison is this secretly nice Shangri-la. That chaos that you hear horror stories about was my new normal. It was going to be a long time before I knew anything other than this.

With knowing the detective in my case tried to use my friends to set me up, I didn't have a good basic trust for police. When I got to prison and witnessed the absolute disregard for human life perpetrated by the correctional officers, my distrust turned into an all-out hate for any law enforcement. The things I would see them do to my fellow prisoners, even murdering them, made me absolutely sick. Then I would look around and see all the different prisoner groups fighting amongst themselves, and it made absolutely no sense to me. If they were going to fight somebody, then fight the common enemy shared by everybody, and not the other prisoners just because they were a different race. Things were the way they were, and they were not going to change anytime soon. All this persecution and hate make the mind grow tired.

There were men having sex with other men everywhere, and they would all swear up and down that they weren't gay. Some had families and would have their wife come and visit them on the weekends, telling them "I love you". They would contract AIDS in prison and spread it to their wife, who had no idea they were sleeping with innumerable amounts of H.I.V. positive men in prison. This pattern is repeated over and over until entire communities have been infected without ever knowing they are carrying the AIDS virus. Men are forced to be sex slaves, even though they aren't gay. Their weakness physically makes them easy prey to the sadistic predators behind bars. People are stabbed, murdered, and raped on a daily basis of never-ending insanity that is called home to many men and women today. This was my home, and this was the environment that I grew up in for ten years of my life. This type of living-where you face the possibility of death on a daily basis for years on end-is never good for the development of a healthy mental state. I was no different since every second of my life was spent with my adrenal glands working at maximum capacity. Your brain can only take so much of this before you completely lose touch with reality. You turn into a savage animal with no morals or semblance of rationality inside you. You turn into a monster, because a monster is the only thing that survives in the middle of a nightmare. You don't want to most of the time-you just have to.

Eventually, all this negativity gets too hard to bear on your own. Most people do what I eventually did, which is turn to drugs to numb the pain. You would think that drugs would be hard to come by since you are locked up in a cage, but sadly the prison guards are just as corrupt as the killers they are keeping watch over. With very rich organized crime heads offering you thousands of dollars to bring in drugs that you can hide in your pocket, it was also very hard to deny the temptation to make that kind of money for so little work. This made the access to drugs very easy for those who had the right connections. People knew I was a very loyal person and that I could be trusted since I was a killer who hated cops. This gave me easy access to all the major drug supplies in the prison. I took full advantage of this privilege and chose to self medicate myself all day, every day, with almost every narcotic I could get my hands on.

Sadly, the drugs don't take away loneliness. Loneliness I know because prison is one of the loneliest places on earth. It is a different kind of being alone. You can't talk to people when you want to talk. Just to make a phone call, you have to plan days in advance. Even then you aren't guaranteed that your family will be home to accept your call. Writing letters takes about a month to get where it is mailed. The response is usually so outdated there was no point to write the letter in the first place. This is the problems with the communication you are allowed to have. Apart from visits, which are the best of all the options, you have absolutely no contact whatsoever with the outside world. When you are having a hard day there is no one to turn to. When life is hard you just have to stick it out silently. The type of loneliness you feel is almost a deep type of grieving. Like the pain you feel when a loved one really close to you dies unexpectedly. At least then you have other loved ones to help bear the burden of grief. Prison is worse than even this feeling. It's almost as if every person you have ever known is unexpectedly killed in one massive accident. One day you have everyone you care about in life, and then the next they are torn from your hands in an instant. No goodbyes, no I love you, and worst of all, no closure. Only a life time of regrets, coupled with the fact that you have no chance to try and make things right, even if you wanted to. It is the most desolate feeling on earth. It certainly doesn't help that all the while you are dealing with this inside the most hostile environment on earth. I believe it is a miracle that anybody can keep their sanity living under those conditions.

Let me try and explain about how sorry the food, clothes, and toiletries situation is in prison. First off, there are times that you have to wash your own clothes in the toilet of your cell. These toilets almost certainly have a minimum of two deadly viruses growing in them at all times. You go to the bathroom in the morning, and then wash your clothes in the same place later that day. It is absolutely disgusting, but you have to do whatever you have to do in there. The clothing itself has been worn by probably at least one hundred other people before it hits your hands. They do buy new clothes often, but on average many people have worn the clothes before you. This is not good, because many prisoners are H.I.V. positive or have tested positive for Hepatitis C. Lice, Crabs, and every type of rash imaginable are mixed in with the feces and semen deposits left over from gay sex in the clothing. Why? Well, because all the clothes are washed together in a communal washing machine. This is the reason many people opt to just wash their clothes in the toilet instead of sending them to the ironically dirtier washing machine. The whole concept is putrefying to think about, I know, but it is the reality you live with. The quality of the food itself isn't half bad, believe it or not. Don't get me wrong, technically a lot of people hate it, and will tell you it is the worst tasting stuff on earth. Most of the time it is made from animal bi-products which are shipped from the same places that dog food suppliers order their food. I know all this to be true, but I need to compare our treatment in the prisons in America with the treatment in other countries to properly be taken in context. There are places in Mexico where the only food you get is a couple of old molded loaves of bread, and the leftover fish guts from the market which are not refrigerated for safety purposes. Even with this, there isn't enough for everyone to eat, so you have to fight for the little bit of nasty scraps that they throw in to you. The biggest problem with the American prisons is that you get such small portions that you are in a perpetual state of starvation. You have enough food to survive, but it is just barely enough to survive. You stay almost always a tiny bit sick from starvation at all times, but healthy enough to technically live through the day. Also, in prison you can't go to the local grocery store and buy what you need to keep yourself clean. If it isn't sent in by your family, you don't get nice things. This is a luxury most prisoners are not blessed with. You are not even guaranteed a shower every day since people get killed all the time, with everyone getting locked in their cells for months at a time. It's also not a good idea to be dirty in an environment where so many diseases and deadly viruses are running around rampant. This is another reason why things spread so fast from prisoner to prisoner. Long story short, prison is a dirty, disgusting place to live your life, so don't ever purposely put yourself in a situation where you might end up here.

My next ranting about my experience in prison is the entire lack of privacy. This is an understatement when I say lack of privacy. The wall of privacy, or any sense of it, is demolished in prison. Your first experience with this is when you are strip searched. To make sure you are not sneaking any contraband or weapons into the facility, you must endure these searches on a regular basis. You strip down naked in front of the guards to start. Then you must open your mouth and show that you are not hiding anything in your hair. The next step is you lift your testicles to show nothing is hidden in that space either. You finish off this emasculating experience by bending over to spread your butt cheeks and coughing to let them know you don't have anything inside your person. I think that's the least gross way to explain the whole process. I have personally been the victim of literally thousands of these searches in my lifetime. Another very cool experience you will partake in is taking a shower. Let me give it to you straight-in prison, you will be taking every shower with other men inches away. You have to get over any modesty you possess awfully quickly in that place. So if you think going to prison is cool because only tough gangsters go there (people actually believe this by the way), remember that you will be taking showers everyday with thousands of other naked men. That's what you have to look forward to if you think a life of crime is a cool life to pursue. On top of all this, you are never alone at any time. When you are sleeping other people are there. When you are taking a dump or going to the bathroom in any way people are inches away, carrying on a conversation with you. From changing clothes to brushing your teeth, you are never alone in prison. This is probably the most frustrating thing because you never have silence either in prison. The place is stressful enough with the violence and the danger. You never have a break at any time, because you are never alone. There are times you just want to relax for a second and just take a few deep breaths to get your head on straight, but that option doesn't exist. Your only option is to compound all your built up stress and anger with more built up stress and anger. It never stops piling onto your psyche, because you never have a time to process all the old problems that you are building up day after day.

Then you have to deal with all the unwritten racial prison laws, and punishment thereof, if you are a prisoner. The most racist people on earth are in prison. The most racially segregated places on earth are in prisons. Everything is dependent on what racial background you belong to. That has the first and last say as to all things you can do in prison. The first thing both the guards and the other prisoners ask you is your race. Your identification card says what race you are. The prisoner who you bunk up with has to be the same race as you. Who you walk with has to be the same race as you. Who you eat with has to be the same race as you. Who you talk to has to be the same race as you. This extends to all avenues of your social life, and the law is ultimate and unchangeable. At the same time, the punishment of violation of this said law is also ultimate and unchangeable. No matter how small a matter, all the punishments are about the same. Easiest of the punishments is that you get beat down so badly you must take a trip to the intensive care unit because you might not live through the night. This usually leaves you permanently handicapped and bound to a wheel chair for the rest of your life. They also can choose that you will live the rest of your stay in prison as not only a woman, but a sex slave to boot. I emphasis this choice is made for you, completely against your will. You have to act like a woman, dress like a woman, and you have to wear makeup made from skittles candy and kool aid. If you resist, they just gang rape you so many times that eventually you just give in and live your life as a homosexual. The last and most common resort is you are just murdered in the most violent fashion imaginable. Some people are thrown off tiers that can be up to five stories tall. Some people are stabbed so many times they resemble human Swiss cheese. You can have your throat cut from ear to ear, and it goes all the way down to being hanged in your cell. The possibilities are endless as long as it is a violent, painful, and extremely bloody death. The punishments seem very severe, but with such absolute consequences to your actions this tends for the most part to keep order within the racial classes. Most of the riots and violence of prison are brought against the other racial backgrounds that you don't belong to, for the simple purpose that they are not the same race as you. Other than that, there is no other explanation as to the hate that goes on in prison.

In short, prison is chaos manifested by the most violent people on earth. There is no rhyme, reason, or rest for your body and mind. It turns good people into monsters, and bad people worse. This is my life.

CHAPTER 10: MY CURSE OF DESOLATION

For years I drowned myself in pity and hatred with drugs and alcohol. Pills and other narcotics were what I ate instead of food. My only friend was the hate for humanity that came everywhere I went. The two of us were inseparable. As far as I was concerned my life was over, so I might as well do all the drugs I could get my hands on. I gained massive amounts of weight and went into a deep depression that lasted at least five years. From 2002 until 2005, I don't think I even faced one day that entire time. As soon as I would wake up, I would get so high I would pass out most of the day, and when I eventually woke up, I would take more drugs and sleep the remainder of the day. It was like this for three or four years. I was frozen in a time capsule while the rest of the world passed me by. I might wake up a few minutes to eat when I was hungry, but seconds later I would get high and pass out. I wasn't even really alive during this time period.

I think that in a backwards attempt to not be lonely during this period, I purposely chose to spiral downward into my worst personal mental illness episode ever. Night after night, I would have hour long conversations with my other personalities. I knew well that the more I let them out the stronger they would become, but at this point I just didn't care anymore. A part of me actually wanted them to be stronger so that I never had to live my life again. Maybe one of them could just take over forever this time. Inside my mind I created a literal room with a table in the center where we would conduct our brain trust meetings with each other. We needed somebody to pay for what had been done to us. We needed the most primal revenge ever lusted for by a human being. We were supposed to end up having a life of walking greatness. It was our destiny to end up powerful and wealthy with the world held down in our strangle hold. Now we have been reduced to less than nothing. There was only one solution for the great injustice done to my psyche. Everyone involved would pay for their sin against us. Thinking of how I would hurt these people was like a fun game that I would use to pass the time… and I had plenty of time to think of how to destroy my enemies.

The first plan of action was to determine who would receive vengeance for my betrayal. There were a lot of obvious choices for this list, but the short list quickly became very long as I thought of everyone to blame for what happened to me. Only one name actually deserved to be on this list however. Of course I wasn't at the place yet to realize or even recognize that the only person to blame for my life results was me. I was too steeped into my own self pity to actualize this simple truth. In the meantime I would continue to make a list a mile long of all the people to blame for my current living conditions. Not only had I been betrayed by those who dared to call me a friend, but I had been the center of an elaborate police conspiracy to frame me for a crime I wasn't guilty of. Even when they found me guilty, they blatantly abused their power further by sentencing me to an exaggerated 11 years in prison. It wasn't fair that my friends ratted on me only to save their own skin from serving jail time. It wasn't fair that the court system used me as a pawn in their attempt to gain personal political power by getting a conviction in a high profile criminal case. It wasn't fair that my destiny was interrupted by cowards who would sell their own mother down the river to weasel out of true justice being served. None of this was fair, it just wasn't fair. For years the other personalities and I planned the most violent revenge that our twisted brains could think of. This was the pathetic reality that was my life during this dark period.

Somehow my mind needed to come to the terms that, at best, my revenge would be waiting for at least another ten years. I then came up with the plan to pacify my immediate need for blood by taking it out on the people I hated almost as much as the betrayers who called themselves my friend. I began to trade around the idea with other inmates how we shouldn't have to take the treatment we were receiving from the cops. By planting these seeds in the minds of very violent men I had hoped to start a riot against cops. At best, maybe some of the guards would be killed in martyrdom for my cause. On the surface I tried to make it a humanitarian effort so that we would end the mistreatment of prisoners. The fact of the matter was I needed to satisfy the bloodlust that boiled inside me day after day. When my plans weren't met with the enthusiasm I had first anticipated, it made me even more hateful towards the inmates around me. They would talk a big talk but when it came down to walking the walk, they were scared to not be able to go home when their term was up. I called them cowards in my heart and knew that once again my attempts for revenge had been foiled. What was I going to do now?

I was beginning to realize the futility of my plans for revenge. I was helpless to do anything about all the hate that I was holding inside. I had no outlet for years of built up frustrations that I was heaping upon my mind. All I thought about every second of the day was how unfair this all was, and how much I hated the people who put me here. I couldn't leave my literal and mental cell that I was being held in. All I wanted was to hurt the people in charge of ruining my life, but every day I was stuck in this cage. The days turned into weeks, which turned into months, which turned into years, which turned into more years. This was when I realized that the revenge that I lusted over all these years was not going to happen. With the amount of drugs I was doing on a daily basis, there was a good chance I probably wasn't going to live through prison. It was likely that there would be an overdose in my near future. Obviously, my response to this frustration was to only do more drugs than before to numb the pain. Every cell in my body was saturated with hate and a need to kill anyone remotely responsible for my life in prison. At the same time I was completely helpless to act on these emotions, so I just did drugs, drugs, and more drugs. It was such a pathetic display of humanity that thinking about it to this day still makes me sick to my stomach.

Something had to give and I knew I couldn't just continue doing more drugs since I already went to the edge of overdosing every time I got high. I couldn't do more, but the amount I was taking wasn't working anymore, either. I had tried every mental illness drug imaginable and that didn't work. Nothing was working and I felt worse than ever. I finally tried something that I had never considered before. I don't even know why I came up with this as a possibility, other than I had literally tried everything else in the book already. I would quit doing drugs and live my life as a sober person for the first time ever. I chose to quit cold turkey, which is a really not a fun thing to do when you need to kick a heroin habit. It is bad enough when you quit only heroin, but I was also quitting multiple opiates at very high doses. For the next week I was bedridden with severe pain throughout my body the entire time.

You are cold, then hot, sweaty and then dehydrated. Sleep is impossible, but you are always attempting sleeping. In laymen's terms, it is hell on earth. Once the pains subsided and I was able to function normally again, I felt very proud of the sacrifice that I had gone through for myself. I had forgotten what sober even felt like, but it actually was a good feeling. This wasn't half bad and I had a sense that I would actually make it through this chapter in my life. I had only cured the symptoms, however, and the illness was still with me every step of the way. I had underestimated the fact that the problem itself was not the original cause of that same problem. If I didn't directly treat the cause of the problem, the actually problem will only return stronger than before. This was absolutely true at the first glance of trouble in my life. All it took was one case of stress to enter into my world and I was back off the wagon, with twice the amount of narcotics flowing through my blood stream than any time before. My failed attempt to change life under my own power was a major wakeup call as to how desperately pathetic a human being I really was. I was an absolute piece of trash nothing, who would do the world a favor by ridding it of my existence.

I had now truly, for the first and only time, had finally hit rock bottom. My life was bad when I developed multiple personalities, but it wasn't my rock bottom. My life was even worse when I was threatened with the death penalty, but it wasn't rock bottom. Being sentenced to eleven years in prison even didn't bring me to the place where I hit rock bottom. I had never truly understood what this concept of rock bottom was until I had felt its' disgraceful embrace myself. It is a feeling un-describable by human words. I can't portray now properly just how much of a loser I felt at that moment. One thing was sure at the time, and it was the fact that I was done running things under my own power. I signed up for a special day treatment program in another part of the prison where I would attend group therapy sessions all day, like going to school. More importantly, I would be temporarily cut off from the main line inmates so that I would force myself to get clean, off drugs, cold turkey. That was really as far as my plan went. I wanted God to somehow take over the rest, because I obviously couldn't plan anything good on my own. I wasn't fully surrendering to go out and preach or anything like that, but I just was turning my life over to God. What that meant, I honestly had no idea at the time. This was uncharted territory for me. I had never done anything like this so I didn't really know where this road would lead me. I didn't know if it would be easy or hard to follow God fully. All I knew was this one thing-that I was done. I had simply had enough pain, and I was done.

CHAPTER ELEVEN: A NEW HOPE

I was intimidated by the fact that I wouldn't be calling the shots anymore. I had no idea even where to start. Then I remembered a weird event that had taken place the prior week. I had gotten a pass to go to a church service in the chapel on Sunday afternoon. Now the thing about getting passes anywhere in prison is that there is a long, drawn out process to obtain any pass. It doesn't happen by accident, and just because you ask for one, usually doesn't mean you will get the thing anyway. After you do request one, the guards need to review extensively if they want to let you go to this location. Then you have to hope that the pass actually gets printed out, which is a hit and miss endeavor in and of itself. In the off chance that there isn't a prison riot that week which results in your being locked down, and the guard feels like he wants to let you, then you can go to the event originally requested. With this all being said, for the fact that I did not sign up for this pass to go to the church service, and to this day I have no idea as to who or what it was that got me into that class. God definitely had his hand in the matter with whomever it was that got me the pass that day. Not realizing this was all being led by God, I had decided that this was as good a place to start as any. On a Sunday afternoon one day I headed off to my first Celebrate Recovery meeting, having no idea what this even was.

Shortly after attending my first meeting with the group, I realized that this program is all about healing a broken soul. It doesn't limit its scope to focusing only on drugs and alcohol. Whether you have problems with codependence, overeating, a history of any types of abuse, or even if you are dealing with the inner scars of having your parents be addicted to anything while you were growing up, this is the place to bring you healing. What is the key to successfully bring people healing when so many other programs claim to do the same thing with empty results? What sets this place apart? It is simple; they tap into the only true source of healing that exists anywhere in this universe, God's healing power of love. In this program, we don't pretend that we are doing this under our own power. We also don't hint around the fact that we can't do this on our own without actually coming out and openly giving the credit for our recovery directly to the source that deserves the true credit. In this program, you openly acknowledge that God is the only true reason that we can overcome our past. Without him, we could not continue on living a life of forgiveness free from the pain that so long held us captives. God's power is the only reason we are released from our past bondage and we are not afraid to shout from the rooftops that his love for us is the only reason we can truly move on in any positive direction with our life. After attending only a couple of meetings with the Celebrate Recovery group, I knew that I was finally home in this program. It was God who sent me that pass to come to these meetings.

Once again, I was about to embark on a struggle that I knew all too well, which was getting clean. Time and time again, I had only tasted failure when attempting to conquer this mountain in my life. Honestly, I can't even say that this time felt different. Just like all the times before, I was 100% sincere about never doing drugs again. The only difference was I had never relied on God, with every part of my life in his hands. Even though I was sincere about quitting drugs, I know in the back of my mind that I felt like this would once again be a futile effort. I had no idea if actually trusting God would work, but little did I know at the time that trusting fully in God would transform me in aspects that are unexplainable by human definition. Not only was God about to deliver me from my slavery of drugs, but he would use a miracle to completely erase any temptation to want drugs for the rest of my life. All of these things I once thought impossible were given to me as a result of giving my life into his hands completely. Usually I would give him 99% and keep the last percent for myself, but this had only yielded a long string of self inflicted failures. Only by giving my all could God truly start to transform me in the most miraculous of ways.

The only way I can describe how I felt about going to church on a regular basis is that I was home again. I was whole and complete inside the chapel, and no other place could give me that feeling of content. For the first time in my life I worshipped God in a pure way that did not involve ulterior motives. I was worshipping because I loved God, and nothing else mattered. It felt so good that no drug could compare to the peace inside me. I understood for the first time the real joy that surpasses worldly understanding only obtained through being a Christian. I was hooked and I never wanted to feel any other way than the warm embrace of my savior's arms. I started to see the world differently from that day on. I saw people as people who have flaws and made mistakes due to terrible circumstances that a lot of times they couldn't control. I had empathy for other human beings, and I also began having emotions in general, which was a very new thing for me. I actually cared about things other than myself. All of this was absolutely fantastic, but very weird all at the same time. It felt great to be back in church again.

Another step to changing my life was starting school. I was sitting in my cell one day when a bunk mate of mine had an application for college in front of him. He encouraged me to enroll since I was doing nothing else with my life, so I might as well earn a college degree. I couldn't argue with that logic even if I tried. Besides, I was in the middle of really changing my life, and felt very motivated to move forward any way possible. Once I got out of prison I would need to have some educational training to get ahead in this world, occupationally speaking. I long had wanted to study psychology, but never felt worthy enough to take the first steps in doing so. After carefully looking at the application and seeing that one of the degrees was in Psychology, I knew this was the next phase in my transformation. I quickly contacted the appropriate people and got all the necessary documentation signed. This now had me enrolled in college. This would be the first time I had attended any type of school in almost a decade, so I was a little nervous about how hard this would actually be. I figured I would just start out slowly and go from there. I knew I had all day, every day, to get on track with this project, which gave me the confidence that everything would turn out all right. The biggest hiccup I would face is that essentially I would be teaching myself the different subjects as I was locked literally in a cage with no phone or computer at my disposal. Returning a letter would take a minimum of two months, which was not good, either. Despite all this, I was still determined to do my best and excel to the utmost of my ability. It was slow going, but the units started to add up on my way to my first college degree. I was very proud of myself, as was the rest of my family, for trying to earn a college education behind bars.

What God did with healing my mental health problems is the greatest miracle that he performed in my life. The only person who truly witnessed how impossible my situation had become was me. Let me tell you, a thousand years worth of therapy and medication wouldn't have made a dent toward healing what was broken with me. No power on earth that science has to offer would have done anything to cure me of multiple personality disorder. The fact that this would even happen was so far from my scope of belief that I don't even remember exactly when it was that God healed me in this area of my life. One day I just woke up and thought about the fact that my mental illness had gotten so bad in the past. Then something just clicked in my brain at that moment. I hadn't tried to switch over to one of my personalities in years. In fact when I searched for them in my mind, they weren't there anymore. It was so shocking to then put the dots together: God had healed me from one of the most devastating and completely incurable mental illness conditions this earth has ever known. It still seems impossible to this day that this actually happened. Because this condition only existed within my own mind, I'm the only person who can really grasp the magnitude of this great and powerful miracle. I wish that I could convey with words to everyone what actually happened, but no human words can give this miracle justicè.

Forgiveness is an odd concept. I used to think it was a double-sided thing that both people were involved with. Not only did I find closure with the people who had wronged me, but they needed to make some type of amends for what they did before I could really forgive them. This couldn't be farther from the truth of the real definition of the word forgiveness. Jesus tells us to forgive those who persecute you, and to have joy as this persecution happens. Forgiveness only lies within you, and has nothing to do with the other person. The need for some explanation as to why the other person did what they did is not forgiveness. Besides, most of the time they either can't remember what you are talking about or never knew they wronged you in the first place. The problem with this method is the problem will always lie with you, even when the other party has long forgotten their past sin. Other times, people know they wronged you and don't care what you think about their past. They don't care, and are not sorry on top of that. You will never forgive anything if you need the other person to feel sorry for what they did as a condition of your forgiveness. I would hide behind this false belief for years before I couldn't use it as a crutch anymore. The truth is I didn't want to forgive anyone for what they did to me, because I loved to hate them for it. I couldn't let go of the evil desires that I harbored inside toward those who hurt me. If I forgave them, then I was giving up any chance for revenge. Now this whole philosophy was too much to carry around anymore. It was too big of a burden to bear. There are a lot more people out there that I have wronged than there are people who have wronged me. Now that I was changing my life, I needed some of them to forgive me for all the sins I committed against them. This was not easy to admit, but how can I expect them to forgive me if I can't forgive other people for hurting me? The bible tells a parable of how one man was forgiven debt of approximately 8 billion dollars, but could not forgive a man that owed him about a dollar. Because of that un-forgiveness, he was thrown into prison until he could repay his original debt. Obviously 8 billion dollars is impossible to pay back, so he would stay in prison forever after that.

In church one afternoon, I finally found and accepted my life's calling. A friend of mine, who was one of the teachers in the program, had secretly nominated me for a teacher's position. I had no idea about this, which is probably for the best since I might have declined the offer. With the rapid growth of the program, they were in need of other Godly men to help teach some of the new students coming in. There was a long waiting list starting to form which desperately needed to be accommodated. Another gentleman and I were the two main candidates who would go through the interviewing process. The method used to interview us was a very different one, to say the least. It would happen without our knowing it was even going on. We were simply watched in our daily life to see who didn't change once they left the church. Did we really walk the walk, or were we simply just talking the talk? By God's grace, they saw that even though I was far from perfect, I was really making an attempt to change for the better. That is when the other elders pulled me into the church office and offered me the new teaching position which was available. My first instinct was to say no immediately, which they had already anticipated. They let me know they would be there with me every step of the way. This was very comforting since I was just about as nervous as I had ever been. I also had known for a very long time that this is what God really wanted me to do. I trusted in God that he would take care of me and happily accepted the position. I took baby steps in getting my feet wet, helping by reading bible verses in front of everyone. Then every once in awhile, I would get up and share a few thoughts on some Bible verses. Once I started to gain confidence in what I was doing, I dove into the leadership training to get ready for the real deal. Finally the day arrived where I would take over my new class.

To explain what I was up against in this new endeavor is a little hard for people who don't understand the environment of the class. I was a 25 year old kid trying to teach the Bible to people twice my age. Not only that, but they were prisoners who hated authority anyway, and most of them used to kill people over the slightest gesture of disrespect. They hated being told what to do, and now some young kid who never had taught a class in his life, let alone the deep intricacies of God's word, was about to be given power over what they studied. Needless to say, I had a monumental task in winning over their trust and respect as a teacher. Obviously I had to put this in God's hands fully so it would not become a total failure. With the guiding of the Holy Spirit, they gave me a chance, and slowly they saw the genuine love in my heart. We grew into a family that was so close that we would die for each other. We had a bond as brothers that would never be broken. I was angry that all these years I had run from the one thing that would make me feel most content.

I was beginning to feel self worth for the first time in years. It felt very weird and different, as did most of my new emotions. The easiest way to explain my new self worth was that I didn't wish to die every living second of my life. Death was a friend to me who I wished would finally visit me, and end all this suffering I had always lived with. Every day of my life was the worst day of my life, and all I wanted constantly was to die. Now that I had given my life over to God, I slowly had these feelings drifting away. There were some days that I actually liked living. Other days I was proud of what I had accomplished with the time given me in life. I couldn't believe I was feeling like this, but I was truly happy to be alive. Working down at the church and helping other prisoners find peace in life was the secret for my own mind to find peace. I had never put anyone before myself, and now all I did was help other people. It was the most freeing and relaxing experience to me. Finally I understood what it meant to find rest in the Lord. All the years of looking over my shoulder and running was finished at last. What I was running from was actually the very thing I should have been running toward. Finally, I was in the bosom of my Father who, after all these years, gave me the gift of his rest.

One of the greatest side effects of all this new happiness was my family being able to see the real difference in my life. They could only see me about every three months or so at the most, but that was enough time to notice the drastic changes in my character. I don't think anyone else could see such a physical difference in the way I carried myself other than my mother, who visited me most often. When I first was locked up, we were barely able to carry on a conversation with each other. I didn't want to hug her and I couldn't say I love you to her, because I didn't. Now all she had to do was look into my eyes to see how much I cared about her, and that was only possible by the changes that God made in my life. I remember only wanting my mother to someday be proud of me when I was growing up. Now I finally knew for a fact that she was proud of the person that I was becoming. I never would be able to accomplish that on my own, apart from God taking over my life. As time went by and my mother was able to tell the rest of my family how much I had changed, more and more people would start to visit me. Now the rest of my family saw firsthand that I really had changed, and they, too, gave me a second chance to be back in their life. Other family members whom I hadn't seen in almost eight years were making a ten hour round trip visit to say that they loved me, and had never stopped praying for me. The people who could not make it in person would write to tell me how thankful they are to God for answering their prayers that He would help me get on the path I was currently walking. All this support meant more to me than anyone will ever understand who hasn't lived in prison for as long as I had. You are so alone and isolated to the point where you don't think anyone knows or cares that you are still alive. This makes you not care if you are alive, physically or mentally, and it makes it very easy for your mind to just check out from itself while inside prison. To have outside love and support from people who care about you is paramount in keeping your humanity in the most inhuman environment on earth. As weird as it sounds, before then I never felt like I was part of a family. Now for the first time, I didn't just feel, but I knew I had a family. The joy I felt because of my family fact so uplifting that I was able to stay focused on the task at hand, which was continuing to stay clean of drugs and keep my eyes on God's plan for me.

The last and most complex of the changes that were happening in my life is that I felt there was a possibility of finding love in my future, and that I was actually worthy to receive it. Of all the positive changes, I think I feared this one the most. All of my problems were centered on my fear of trusting people. I would rather feel no emotions at all than give anyone the remote chance of hurting me again. Things were different now in my life. I felt like a good person for the first time ever. For the first time, I felt like I did deserve nice things to happen to me. Things were different, and I knew happiness was out there for me, also. As much as I knew all these things, it scared me just the same. I would have to put myself out there emotionally for someone else and this is something I was just not used to doing. All these past hurts and hang ups are what I continued to work on in the Celebrate Recovery program. Slowly, with the help of God every step of the way, I started to confront the demons of my past that were holding me down from the life I wanted to live. This was directly tied into every aspect of my life. The roots were not easy to pull out because of how deeply they had actually grown. Almost every waking moment in my life I worked to overcome the years of walls that I had put up. Some days were good, filled with triumph over my past. While others were so depressing that I felt like giving up and living my old lifestyle, because it was easier than confronting my past. God was there, however, and with his help once again, I was able to tell the mountains in my life to jump into the sea. Like clockwork, every mountain had to obey the word of God, and one by one, they all threw themselves into the ocean.

CHAPTER TWELVE: THE ORIGINAL SIN

The Holy Bible states that the root of all evil is the love of money. The original sin lies with the fall of Lucifer from heaven. These two things are intertwined together for eternity. The roots of sin are not loving money specifically, but the power it brings you. Lucifer himself had tasted true power that is only seconded by God's own throne. Power is the single most potent drug that has ever existed in the universe and Lucifer had grown an addiction to its intoxicating lust. He could not get enough and had been limited by the only being more powerful then himself. He lusted for more no matter what the cost even if the price tag was everything. I can sympathize to the weakness Lucifer suffered. I too felt the power of God and lorded this over my fellow humans. I had been given a portion of the Holy Spirit that I have personally never witnessed before. I wasn't ready for this gift and I abused its privileges. God had given me the true and innocent gift of the Holy Spirit and all the responsibility with it. I let the root of evil slither into my soul and my lust for power started to slowly eat at me like a cancer. I was the chosen of God. Nobody else had been given this honor, because nobody else was worthy to receive it. People who were four times my age and had been studying the scriptures their entire lives didn't understand one percent of the bible that I knew. God had chosen me for something bigger than everybody else. Sure they were Christians but I was a chosen prophet of God. It was sad how far I let myself fall under the pretense that God was leading me every step of the way. Something drastic needed to be done and my Father was about to do exactly what needed to be done to bring me back. What happened next was one of the most horrible experiences I have ever faced.

I had this sense of pride that I was a true teacher of God and nobody else knew what they were talking about. Everyone else I thought was basically using their own minds to interpret the bible that's why they had studied for decades and still only knew the basic concepts of scripture. I actually had the Holy Spirit teaching me so I was given secrets in a few years that couldn't be learned over hundreds of years of human study alone. The only way to truly understand the Bible was to let the Holy Spirit be the one teaching it to you. The human mind cannot grasp the heavenly concepts put forth in the Holy Scriptures on its own. It is an impossible task to try and accomplish. I knew this as fact and so I could easily spot that no one else was advancing in knowledge as quick as me because they must not have the Holy Spirit teaching them. If the Holy Spirit wasn't actually teaching them the truth of scriptures then I knew they couldn't be getting the proper interpretation of the gospel. Therefore if they didn't have the true interpretation of the gospel then everything they would try to teach me would be false teachings. I didn't need to be associating with people who were falsely interpreting the bible and trying to call themselves teachers when they didn't even know what they were talking about. After realizing this I pretty much stopped listening to other people who weren't advanced in Christ's knowledge know what would come out of their mouth was probably wrong in the first place. I wasn't going to listen to people who didn't know what they were talking about. After a short period of time I realized nobody knew what they were talking about except me.

Once again during one of the happiest accomplishments for my class I had to make everything about me. They were graduating from the "Purpose Driven Life" course along with another class. When the main leader didn't give my class enough attention during the ceremony I literally was so mad I couldn't speak. How dare he disrespect my class like in that way? If anything we should get more attention because we were actually trying in the courses. Every other class just wanted to look good for the parole board by earning another certificate. They didn't really care about changing their life. Everyone in my class knew I was very upset and tried to calm me down but I would have nothing of it. To them it was no big deal and it really wasn't. The real problem is I thought so highly of myself my pride was wounded when I wasn't shown the proper respect that someone as important as I deserved. To top it off I walked out of the graduation for my own class. That is how self centered I had become. I was drunk with my own sense of being better then everyone around me. All the while I was calling myself a follower of God.

I started getting even worse than that by bragging about all that I was and that God had given his chosen son. I talked on and on about the things that I would have when I left prison. My ministry would be huge, and the sky was the limit because I had God's blessing behind everything that I touched. I would earn a doctorate in college and go to make lots of money helping other people. Blessings would flow down from heaven because God couldn't afford to give my responsibility to anyone other than myself. This is how blind and vain I had actually become in my own mind. It makes me sick to think of all the blasphemy's that I spoke against God. It was like a sports star that could ask for anything he wanted because the team couldn't afford for them to be traded elsewhere. The situation was definitely very sad, but it was truth of what I had become.

What happened next was a direct plea from God to stop my insane behavior. Sadly I heeded not this plea and started my inevitable downfall because of my vain thinking. When this happened, everything was taken away from me that I held dear to my heart. I see now this was necessary so everything that held dear to my heart could be taken away. Why? Everything that held dear was dark and evil in every way possible. In the middle of a normal night's sleep I was awoken in a dream to a loud, clear, and terrifying voice. "No Silver and Gold"! That short statement was sent to me from heaven itself. I knew it was an angel's voice but I can't describe how I knew. Looking back now and reading everywhere in the bible where this statement is made it is clear that this was a warning. A warning to stay away from the pride of the world which I had so deeply found myself attached to. A warning to throw away the things that this world held dear which were represented by silver and gold. My God was pleading that I would release my pride and contempt for my fellow man before it destroyed me from the inside out. Did I heed this warning that was so great God himself sent a messenger from heaven itself to tell me? Of course I did not because I was too far gone in my own glory. I didn't even take it at the time as a warning. I took at as reassurance that I was God's chosen vessel to carry his words to the world. I actually thought it was reassurance that I was doing everything right and to continue on even stronger on the path that I was marching so boldly down. Instead of immediately stopping my blaspheming actions, I turned up the volume 300%. Now I knew I was a true prophet of God because he had come down from heaven himself to reassure my importance and blessings in life. The whole thing is disgusting to me now, and what happened next couldn't come fast enough.

There are a lot of rules you must follow in prison. I started to get this idea that I was so important that those rules didn't apply to me anymore. I also knew that most of the female staff members working there thought I was attractive. Having God backing every move I made, I thought it was a good idea to start openly flirting with the female prison employees. This obviously didn't fly with the other male staff members and I was quickly thrown into the hole for my efforts. The hole is a prison within the prison where you have no contact with other people at all. 24 hours a day you are locked inside a cell by yourself. No TV, radio, or any of the few things you are allowed to have in the first place. You can't interact with other prisoners, which meant I couldn't teach my class anymore either. I had to stop going to college, and couldn't even go to church services with all the other believers. You are completely isolated and have nothing but time to contemplate why you are banished from the rest of the population. For the first time I realized who had actually put me there. God had used my own vain actions to stop me from myself. All of a sudden I realized how wrong I was about thinking I could do anything I wanted, no matter what it was, and still have God's blessing. I was a horrible person and had taken my saviors love for granted like a spoiled little child. I was finally starting to realize just how low I had fallen. God wasn't done with me yet, however, I still had a long way to go before I hit bottom.

Perhaps the worst thing that has ever happened to me came next. Thinking I could just feel sorry for my actions and apologize to God I began to try and pick up where I left off spiritually. The plan was to wait out this little misunderstanding with the police and in a couple of days they would let me out of the hole. Until that happened, for a few days I would study the bible, just waiting to take over my class again as if nothing had happened. I would apologize for my actions and show my students that I stayed very spiritual throughout the lesson that God had taught me. The truth is I wasn't actually sorry at all, so God knew I needed a little extra push to really bring me to my knees in repentance. I picked up my Bible to do my regular daily studies when looking at the words in scripture I realized something very horrible. I no longer understood scripture or anything whatsoever about the bible. I knew nothing that I had known before no matter how basic the bible lesson. God had reached down and taken away the gift that was always his in the first place. I had greatly abused my privileges and so he took those blessings away from me. The moment I realized that God had taken my understanding of scripture away, it was like time stood still. I was so ashamed that he had done that to me. I was a child looking into the loving but disappointed eyes of my father. Knowing that I let him down broke my heart in literal fashion. I began to feel less of the Holy Spirit inside my body. A part of me was taken away and I began to feel the loneliness and self hatred that I had felt before I was saved. A great cloud of depression instantly engulfed every hidden corner of my soul. To feel this way once again was unbearable to me. Once again I turned to only option I knew that would take these feelings away without God's help. I would rather kill myself than feel this way again. Suicide was exactly the plan I was about enact. Not only would I kill myself but I would do it in a way worthy of the suffering that my wretched life deserved. I started to simply starve myself to death. How old habits do die hard?

The guards quickly saw that there was something terribly wrong going on with me. By my distraught demeanor and the fact that I wasn't eating my food they put two and two together. I was sent to the suicide unit where I would be under constant 24 hour surveillance until I stopped wanting to kill myself. Everything that could be used to help kill myself was taken away from me including my clothing. They give you this smock that can't be destroyed to cover yourself with but it isn't much. I was butt naked in the suicide unit with a nurse watching me every second of the day. This was nothing compared to the state of mind that I was in. God had taken most of his spirit from me. I still felt a faint sense of it, but nothing like before. When I tried to read the bible, day after day it was harder to understand than quantum physics to a three year old. I still remembered knowing all the scripture that I would so eloquently teach others. Now when I went to retrieve that information from my brain it wasn't up there anymore. Every day felt worse than the one before. A normal stay in the suicide unit was about two weeks at the most, until you felt like living again. Three months later and I was still as bad off as the first day I came there. Eventually they had to send me back to the hole due to time restraints. I had no outlook of getting any better. Almost a year later, I was still rotting away in the hole. All I had was four concrete walls and my own thoughts to haunt me day in and day out. How could I abuse God's gift to the point where he took all I had away from me? How could I be so sure and so wrong at the same time? Finally I was forced to transfer prisons and hopefully get a new start closer to home.

My hatred and the depression nearly killed all hopes of my future ministry. Arriving at the new prison I really felt like the devil had won. I was completely broken in every aspect of the word. I had no will to live, let alone continue on in this war between good and evil. It was all too much for me and I was done with it all. This was the worst position that I had ever gotten into. I had never felt this defeated before. Turns out it was exactly where God needed me to be at the time.

CHAPTER THIRTEEN: REDEMPTION SONG

Starting out in my new setting, I was a sad shell of my former self. When I first arrived I received a glimmer of hope in all the chaos. My appeal had finally been decided on and there was a 90% chance I would go home early. Maybe I could forget about the past year and finally move on with my life. As usual you should never count your chickens before they are hatched. My appeal was denied, which only sunk me deeper into depression. I started sleeping all day and doing absolutely nothing with my life. I started not caring about anything. Once again I just existed without a purpose waiting for the day to end only to start the same routine tomorrow.

After a couple months of feeling really sorry for myself I was moved to another yard. This place had something different from everywhere else in the new prison. They actually had lots of Christians who were eager to spread the word. I was quickly invited to a bleacher study the same day I arrived. It was something I really missed so I agreed to participate. I hadn't felt that kind of love from a fellow Christian in a really long time. A lot of guilt feelings overcame me from all the trouble I had recently caused God. A part of me felt like I shouldn't be there since I was such a hypocrite. Slowly I was brought back into the congregation body despite all the self pity. After a few days I let myself feel more comfortable and was able to start enjoying the services like old times. After a week I started to get my smile back. It wasn't long before I felt like God could give me another chance and was completely happy again going to church. I wasn't all the way back but I felt in God's good graces again. This alone brought contentment to my soul once again.

I thought my days of teaching the word were over until God forced me to return to the ministry that I helped destroy. It wasn't my choice to do something else in the ministry. This is what I was called for and not to sit quietly on the bleachers minding my own business. I was a teacher and if I was going to be involved with the church then this is the task I would do. I had given up on myself but God had not given up on me. I wanted him to give up on me so I wouldn't have to bear the burden of this task. The problem really was, however, the fact that I needed to get rid of some very harmful personal pride. I kept hoping even beyond all this that I had messed up so bad that God would never call me back into the ministry again. Didn't he know that it would just end up the same way it did last time? Like I said, I was hoping he felt that way, but in reality he knew what he was doing. I think I did, too, deep down, but I was just still scared to accept this massive responsibility back on my shoulders. There was a growing need of bible teachers where we were. The amount of people coming there wanting to seek the word was growing larger than are capacity to help them. New teachers desperately needed to be added. Anyone with past experience or a calling to do so was sought out eagerly. I tried to ignore this call by God to come back to my first love. Over and over, I was asked to help the ministry but my fear paralyzed me. I explained to them how I couldn't be trusted with this type of power and to look for someone else. There wasn't anyone else however and I had years of prior training. I knew what I was doing but I was scared to admit it. Finally I couldn't run from God any longer and his conviction overtook my soul. I accepted their call to help teach a morning bible study on the yard. This was the first step to my redemption.

I met with one the spiritual leaders and expressed my concerns that I was afraid of my own temptations. I had yielded to them before, and at the time, I knew I would be overcome by their powers yet again. He knew about my past, and knew the fact that I was aware of my temptations. He also knew this was the first step in overcoming them. I was humbled by the experience and I didn't want to make the same mistakes. Along with constantly seeking God's advice and guidance, he saw possibilities in me that I refused to recognize. All I was doing was trying make up any excuse in the book not to teach again. My excuses were all weak and had no standing with what God's plan in my life was. Honestly, I was scared to ruin anyone else's spiritual walk due to my own prideful behavior. Eventually, I had to suck it up and step up to the plate.

One day I had to witness the hatred of fellow Christians. This whole situation that I went through was an eye opening revelation. It all started when the Christian body asked someone to start teaching some of the bible studies on the yard. Before he accepted the invitation, he told him that he kept and honored the

Lord's Sabbath day. This instantly brought rage to the faces of those we called brethren. To them this was paramount to blasphemy, since they thought God's law was done away with when he was crucified. Trying to explain that the Ten Commandments were not done away with, since that itself was God's character, we had no luck. We tried to reason together by looking up multiple scriptures saying that we should still follow the Ten Commandments because not doing so is the definition of sin. Legalism is the phrase that continually got pushed down our throats. This was thinking you were saved by following the law, but we didn't believe that at all. We knew there was no other way to be saved besides God's sacrifice for our sins. In short, it didn't matter what we said or showed them from the bible, their ears and eyes were closed to anything we did. They weren't really listening in the first place, so why were we even talking? The whole situation was so sad and depressing. I had been told to watch out for this type of reaction, but I never believed that it would have so much hatred behind it from fellow believers. If they could, they would have stoned us, right then and there. The following days and weeks only brought more division from their end of the brotherhood. It finally got to the point where we weren't welcome in their worship services anymore. We started our own fellowship apart from them. It was still good and many people still flocked towards the truth, but the lessons learned from the event will never leave my mind. I knew this reaction was not an atypical reaction to this subject. It was actually a foreshadowing of the reaction many nations will have to the very same subject. Nothing you try to say, no matter how right, will be welcomed with an open mind or ear. It will be like yelling at a wall in the middle of nowhere. The devil hates God's character and will bring out the vilest reactions in people when you stand up to defend it. I see how and why the reaction toward this subject in the future as predicted in the bible gets as ugly as it does. Before this, I couldn't understand how fellow Christians could murder their own brothers and sisters over which day was the true day of worship. Satan has programmed in this natural reaction to wanting to follow God's character within the sinful nature of man. This is so imbedded into our sinful nature that it is an instinctive reaction to this very subject. As sad as all this sounds, it is sadder that it's all truthful teachings of which we were warned in God's word itself.

During this, I started getting back into the swing of things by teaching again. This time I felt better than ever, doing what I was born to do. I was really nervous before my first class. It was like riding a bike and once I got back in front of the brothers, I was right at home. There was a big difference this time that I didn't experience before. I was enjoying the gift that God gave me. I was never able to be happy and appreciate the fact that people's lives were being helped. The whole experience felt good and pure, as it should have felt in the first place. I had no selfish motivations behind teaching. I wasn't getting a prideful boost to my ego because of the position I held. I simply loved teaching my friends, and helping create better lives for themselves. It just felt good to be a part of that. I knew nothing more or less than being honored that God was using me to further his cause. Like always, you have to donate a lot of your time studying the word to get everything just right. This is good because you're not distracted by life's nonsense, which there is a lot of in prison. I was able to meditate with God and enjoy a pure fellowship with him which I hadn't experienced in years. I was so happy during this time. I am forever grateful to the Christian men on that yard who pushed me when I didn't want to be pushed back into the ministry. God does a lot of things that we don't like at the time we go through them. I needed to go through a bout of trying to kill myself, spend a year in the hole, and lose everything I had, including my gift of teaching, in order to cut off a big chunk of pride in my life. It is not like my life was all peaches up until that point either, but that was the only time I ever felt God withdraw from me spiritually. That type of abandonment was more than I could bear. In actuality, God never left me for one second. He warned me in dream what the consequences of my actions would bring. Even with a warning from heaven itself, I still chose to abandon God from my life. I still believe I was a breath away from committing blasphemy of His Spirit. If I had continued down the path I was on, and God hadn't warned me to stop, I may have ended up like King Saul. With all the things God brought me through in my life, I finally realized that nothing can stand in my path that I should fear. I had looked death in the eye so many times I would never doubt my Father ever again.

Finally after ten years of living hell, I reached a time that I thought would never come. It is hard to put how it felt in words. I was overjoyed at the fact I was going to leave prison. Then on the other hand, it was all I ever knew. I had friends there that were closer than brothers, who I would never see again. The only place I ever found peace was within those walls. I knew I wouldn't come back, but the fear was always in the back of my mind. How could I be happy if my friends are stuck in Hell? Would I ever fully be able to enjoy my freedom I had worked so hard to reach? I realized I hadn't done this on my own, and all my friends inside didn't make it through the day alone, either. We did it together and now I was leaving them behind. I felt like I was betraying them to be honest. Even now on the other side, I can admit that it is hard to enjoy certain holidays and happy events because I know the torment my brothers are enduring every day. Despite this, I was happy that my mother would once again have peace that her baby boy would be alright. She didn't have to wonder if this was the day someone killed her first born child. Seeing my family as I walked through the prison gates was humbling. Just like I didn't go through this without my friends inside, I was not the only one in prison. My mother and the rest of my family were stuck in there with me. Not in the same way, but they were trapped mentally behind bars. It was as much a release of their souls as it was for mine. Going home was one of the greatest days of my life. I felt like the prodigal son returning from his exile. My father threw a giant feast and I was showered with love and adoration. Great gifts were poured onto my lap as I took in the peace of returning home to the ones I loved so much.

CHAPTER FOURTEEN: RETURN FROM OZ

Coming back to the real world I realized how backwards everything was in my life. Un-normal was normal to me, and the normal seemed like taking a trip to an alien planet. I felt so out of place when I finally got out of prison. As much as I hated every second that I lived there, it was all I knew. I knew how to live around death and despair. I didn't know how to deal with unlocked doors and free will. People on the outside walked way too closely to you which usually meant they were trying to kill you. You're supposed to react to this threat before they get the chance. Out here walking too close to someone just meant they wanted to get to the shampoo aisle at the store. At the grocery store, announcements would be made over the loud speakers and I would freeze with every muscle in my body tense from fear. Why? Well, announcements over the loudspeaker in prison meant there was a riot and you could be about to die. On the outside I told everyone I was fine and just happy to be home. Inside a part of me actually wanted to go back behind bars. It was all I knew and nothing out here seemed right to me.

I felt angry at people because they would tell me they had problems, and they weren't problems at all. I knew what real problems were and it would piss me off to see these people worrying about things that had no impact on their life. People would say they were hungry and had nothing to eat while they could have lived off what was in their fridge for months. I knew what it was like to actually have nothing to eat. No matter what there was nothing in my power that could enable me to obtain food and I just had to starve. People out here had plenty to eat and just didn't want it, so they said they had nothing to eat. This attitude irritated me to no end. Nobody said excuse me when they bumped into you. In prison, if they did this I was completely justified to stab them for their disrespect. I was so out of place it was really a sad sight to behold. Even though I was aware and tried to prepare myself for such differences so that I wouldn't overreact to them, it was still terribly difficult to make the adjustment back to normal life. The task seemed so huge at some points it scared me to where I felt like giving up.

I made sure despite all this pressure to use every avenue at my disposal to succeed in this transition. I went to church immediately upon getting out and surrounded myself with positive Godly people. I forced myself to reach out to others when I would feel uncomfortable in my own skin. I wasn't going to isolate myself only to return to the hell that I once knew. I quickly got connected with a church. I connected with two churches to be exact. This kept me grounded with constant positive influences which wouldn't let me be picked off by the devil's temptations. I knew what I was up against so I protected myself accordingly with God as my rear guard. I knew if I stuck with this plan I would have nothing to worry about. This was easier said than done, however. I had long ago put myself at the top of Lucifer's most wanted list.

One of the greatest joys of my life was teaching the truth of scripture to my family. Soon after my release, we started a bible study every Thursday at my mother's house. I would help teach different lessons and I was having the time of my life. Fellowshipping with my family in God's love instead of trying to tear each other's heads off was a surreal experience to me. It felt really weird, but it also felt right at the same time. Seeing how proud my mother was of me is the most satisfying thing I've ever been a part of. I loved them so much, and for ten years I couldn't spend time with them until now. It puts into perspective what is actually important in life. After ten years there was nothing I wanted to do more than study God's word with the most important people in the whole world to me.

Meeting the love of my life was the greatest gift God ever gave me. She is a part of me the same as my body. She is my moral compass and will to live all wrapped in one. I have no secrets with her because she knows everything about my past, present, and future. I am nothing without her and it is hard to remember life before I met her. It's almost like I wasn't truly living until she became a part of my life. Now that we are married forever, I feel like life has actually begun. She understands me like nobody ever has and that means I can always be my true self with her. She accepts the good with the bad, and I do the same with her. We got married really quickly, but that doesn't make the love story any less magical. Being away from her would be like ripping my own heart out. I love her so much I can't express it enough with a million pages of love sick ranting. Our wedding was so nice. We got married in my parent's giant back yard on a weekend when it was supposed to rain. Like a gift from God, on our wedding day the skies parted, revealing the purest blue sky you could ever imagine. The day was so perfect it should be its own poem. I wondered why God would bless a person the way he had with the past that I possessed. I learned a lesson of how far his love encompasses even those like me who deserve nothing but him turning his back on our life. For the first time I had a real family and this was the best feeling in the world.

About three months after we started dating, I was sent a picture of positive pregnancy tests on my phone. Surprise! I was going to be a father. The joy and fear made me numb. Was I going to be a good father or would I just completely mess this up? The joy definitely outweighed the fear. The responsibility to take care of the baby also hit me like a ton of bricks. I really needed to find a job so I could take care of my new family. We started going to doctors appointments to check on the health of the baby. Not having any real health care, we pretty much got the bottom of the barrel. We just had to stay positive that at least we had something. A few months into the pregnancy my wife was diagnosed with a giant gall stone that was a quarter the size of her entire gallbladder. This brought lots of constant pain on her poor body. Normally she would take pain killers and they would remove the stone right away. Being pregnant put a monkey wrench in the normal treatment of her condition. She had to just tough out the pain and wait around eight months until after the baby was born to have her gallbladder removed. I felt so bad for how uncomfortable she was all the time. We frequently had to make emergency room trips to help relieve the discomfort. In a time where a woman usually eats whatever she wants' my poor wife was on a strict diet. She is one tough cookie, and proved it day in and out during her pregnancy. After nine months of agony, my wife gave birth to our daughter. I was so scared that I would really mess this up. A human life depended on me for everything. I couldn't only worry about my own problems anymore. My daughter trumps anything I think is a problem for the rest of my life.

One of the most frustrating things I encountered was looking for a job with three strikes against me. The first problem being that the current economy made for very few jobs in the first place. Those few people who were lucky to receive jobs needed good resumes and tons of experience. I was bringing exactly none of those things to the table. The second strike against me was obviously my notorious criminal record. I wasn't just having petty crimes show up when people ran my background check. They would see that I had been convicted of manslaughter which doesn't raise a lot of positive flags with employers. The last problem I had for finding a job was my new found religious zeal. More precisely, the fact that I couldn't work Saturdays because I honored the Sabbath really turned employers off. All they see is that I am coming up with a fake excuse to not work weekends. This to them means I am lazy or I like to party a lot. You put these three very negative things together and I had the perfect storm situation of not getting hired anywhere. For eight months day in and day out I tried to get a job anywhere. If they felt like overlooking the criminal history they needed me to work Saturday. If I found a place that would give me Saturday off then when they ran my background check it was a no go. If both of those things weren't a problem, then they only were accepting applications and didn't know when they would be hiring again. I had been going to college to get a degree in Psychology which I thought would really help. I actually got a local drug counseling place to offer me a job but I had to decline because they wouldn't budge on the Sabbath. Another place wanted to start me out in an assistant manager's position, but I couldn't get them to budge on the Sabbath either. Both of these incidents left me in a crying, depressed mess. It didn't help my relationship either, since I kept denying job offers with a child on the way. Eight months of praying and crying to God with no answer in sight. I felt like giving up so many times I can't even count the number. Maybe budging on the Sabbath did start to cross my mind but I couldn't bring myself to do that to God. I knew how important this was to him, and he would honor my dedication in the end. I kept the faith that this would happen. Even if it didn't, I wouldn't turn my back on God. Then one day out of the blue someone gave me a chance. It was one of my biggest answered prayers I had ever received. I praise God to this day because there is no doubt with all the resistance that I faced for this to finally work out for me was his direct hand in my life. The timing couldn't be better since I got the job only a week before my daughter was born.

My darkest hour began like any other day. The only thing different is this weird feeling I had been getting for the past couple days. It was like the Holy Spirit was telling me to watch out for something. I didn't really know what to look out for or why. I was keeping all my spider senses at a high level. My daughter had been coughing the past week, and was beginning to get a fever. It wasn't anything to worry about, though. All of a sudden my wife says that her coughing isn't getting better, so she is going to call the ambulance. Evidently she had been getting the same warnings I had been having. I thought an ambulance was a little drastic because she didn't seem that sick. She was still laughing and playing except she had a fever while she was doing it. Her temperature was 99 degrees when we called the ambulance. When they arrived she was still laughing and the paramedics didn't think anything was wrong with her, but they took her in to check her out anyway. Ten minutes later when they arrived at the hospital, her fever had jumped to 105 degrees. Initial tests showed that her blood had turned poisonous and was septic. Her kidneys were failing and there was a very small chance that she would live past the next couple days. It happened that quickly and without any warning. Suddenly the entire weight of the world hit me like a ton of bricks. The situation didn't seem real. The doctors immediately started the strongest antibiotics that they had available. Further tests needed to be done so they could isolate the exact bacteria that caused the blood infection in the first place. Hopefully they were using the right antibiotics but that was just a guess. If not, there was a good chance she would die. My daughter was only three months old and I was about to lose her. In my entire life I have never hurt as bad as I did during this time. I had never loved anything so much before to let myself hurt this much.

For two weeks she stayed in the hospital hooked up to all kinds of wires and tubes. The whole time she kept a smile on her face. No matter how much pain she was in, she was always smiling. I blamed myself for the whole incident. Karma was finally catching up to me for all the people that I had hurt. Now it was my turn and it was taking away what was most important to me. I was almost afraid to pray because of all the bad things I had done in my life. Maybe this was God's justice coming back to haunt me. I felt this anger inside me that I hadn't known for years. It was this primal hate that I haven't felt since before I gave my life to God. I started to shut down my emotions like I used to do as a teenager. Seeing the stupid looks on people's face made me want to bash their brains in. Everything pissed me off and I wanted to hurt someone for no reason all the time. My mind started to feel numb all the time. This was not a good time for me.

I started having a detachment from reality. I was angry at work and my performance there went downhill really fast. I was angry at home and started not talking to my wife who was spending every moment at the hospital. My daughter could die at any moment and I couldn't do anything about it. I didn't want to admit it out loud but I was also angry with God. I was starting to have a nervous breakdown from the pain I was going through. At last, after a couple weeks the doctors told us they had guessed the right antibiotics and she was receiving the proper medicine the entire time she was in the hospital. The infection had also cleared from her blood after a grueling fight from her 3 month old immune system. Most full grown, healthy adults die when they receive this type of illness, but our new born baby lived through it. When the whole brush with death was over, I held on to my feelings of detachment. All of it really messed me up psychologically and even though my daughter was safe, I didn't want to get close to anything. If I got close to anything like the way I loved my daughter, then if it was taken away I wouldn't feel the hurt I felt in the hospital. It is difficult to explain but I was scared to love something I might lose. My solution was the same as when I was a scared little boy-I chose to love nothing. I am ashamed to say it but that's what I did. In the following months I would isolate myself and push away my wife to the brink of divorce. After all that I went through in prison I still hadn't learned a thing about life. Now I would start my second road to redemption which would be tougher than the first.

I possess a promising and bright future ahead of me in life. My story is far from over, even though this book is coming to a close.

With all the dark storm clouds that I have already passed through, I look forward to the tropical skies in front of me. I've been on a journey and learned life lessons that most people never receive in a hundred years on this earth. I consider my horrible past a blessing and wouldn't change a thing. If I even changed one second of the misery that I lived through, then it would always lead down a road that doesn't end where I presently sit. Therefore, if anything leads away from the perfect happiness and blessings that I now posses then I want nothing of it. I have many regrets but God used my mistakes to shape the person I am today and am becoming in the future. Therefore, when it is all said and done, I wouldn't change a thing.

Made in the USA
San Bernardino, CA
22 March 2014